FIREFL

GUIDE TO THE
STATE OF THE
WORLD

FIREFLY BOOKS

A FIREFLY BOOK

Published by Firefly Books Ltd. 2005

First printing

Publisher Cataloging-in-Publication Data (U.S.)

Wright, John D.
   Guide to the state of the world / John D. Wright.
[208] p. : col. ill., photos., maps ; cm.
Includes bibliographical references and index.
Summary: Practical overview of global politics, economics, environment and culture. Key statistics presented in over 250 specially created maps, diagrams and charts.
ISBN 1-55407-114-3
1. World politics—21st century. 2. Economic geography—21st century. 3. Environmental policy—21st century. I. Title.
909.829 dc22   D862.W754

National Library of Canada Cataloguing in Publication

Wright, John D., 1953-
   Guide to the state of the world / John D. Wright.
Includes bibliographical references and index.
ISBN 1-55407-114-3
   1. World politics—21st century. 2. Economic history—21st century.
3. Civilization, Modern—21st century. I. Title.
D860.W75 2005   909.83   C2005-901362-1

Published in the United States by
Firefly Books (U.S.) Inc.
P.O. Box 1338, Ellicott Station
Buffalo, New York 14205

Published in Canada by
Firefly Books Ltd.
66 Leek Crescent
Richmond Hill, Ontario L4B 1H1

Published in the United Kingdom by Philip's
a division of Octopus Publishing Group Limited
2–4 Heron Quays, London E14 4JP

Printed in China

Front cover
Top left: Human Migration map detail
Centre: Ozone hole in the northern hemisphere
(Greg Shirah/GSFC/NASA)
Top right: Population Growth map detail
Bottom right: Globe in relief
Bottom left: Blue Hmong tribal children in a classroom, Nong Hoi, Thailand
Lindsay Hebberd/*Corbis*
Back cover
Left: Soy plant and bean
Right: Snow leopard

Contents

INTRODUCTION

An understanding of the world we live in necessarily involves a spatial mode of thinking. The *Guide to the State of the World* offers a valuable gateway into important and fascinating aspects of the world today. It undertakes the unenviable task of mapping the contemporary world in an accessible, comprehensive, and comprehensible manner without papering over its complexities. States as recognized political entities lies at the core of the state of the world today – it is difficult to imagine a global humanity without taking into consideration the division of people living in separate states. And yet, the condition of what some call 'globalization' offers us an opportunity to move beyond states and look at flows of people, goods, services, and ideas that do not always respect state boundaries. This *Guide* seeks to provide a glimpse at the interaction between states and highlights the crucial aspects of the world.

When looking at the world political map, one should not forget that the jigsaw puzzle view of the world (with clearly defined state boundaries and each state color coded differently) does not fully capture the complex reality of people and communities that live in the world. People's sense of identity often does not correspond neatly with the state boundaries. Yet, this is the dominant way in which the political map of the world is drawn and hence most issues raised in this *Guide* make sense if understood in terms of state boundaries. Some such issues include various aspects of governance (at the national and international level), human population (absolute numbers, quality of life, livelihood, diversity), and violence (crime and conflicts). On the other hand, other issues in the world require us to complement state level view with a recognition of its international dimensions (for instance, the problems of environment, global political economy, communications and information technology).

In this *Guide*, the short commentaries accompanied with clear maps and figures make the understanding of the world a lot more interesting. There are five interrelated stories one can draw from the maps and commentaries.

First, the world is immensely diverse and complex. Second, extreme levels of inequality mark the contemporary world. This is most clear in the economic sphere. The majority of the world suffers from deprivation and poverty and yet a sizable privileged minority (mostly in the developed countries but also a small powerful elite in the developing countries) live in an abundance of resources. It is this minority that controls the decision-making processes in the world and sets the agenda. Third, diversity and inequality does not undermine the fact that we are living in an interdependent world. Events in one part of the world affect other parts of the world and communication and information technology is playing an increasingly vital role in making us aware of this interdependence. The sooner we realise that the fate of humanity lies not just in the hands of a selected few states, but in the hands of all people living in all states, the better it will be to work together for an international solution to global problems. Fourth, violence against various groups of people is an important feature of the world. States not only face violence from terrorism and war, but they often commit violence with more lethality than nonstate violence. Awareness of the various forms of violence is a good first step toward attempts by individuals to strive for a better, less violent world. Fifth, violence and inequality raise questions about the effectiveness of current political communities. Do we need to imagine a world that moves beyond a state based governmental system? Can we imagine such a world? These are some questions that people need to explore in the future. A *Guide to the State of the World* written a few decades later will be different from this one. For the time being, individual readers need to see what different stories they excavate from this lucidly written, clearly presented, painstakingly researched collection of facts about the state of the world today.

Dr Dibyesh Anand
University of Bath, UK

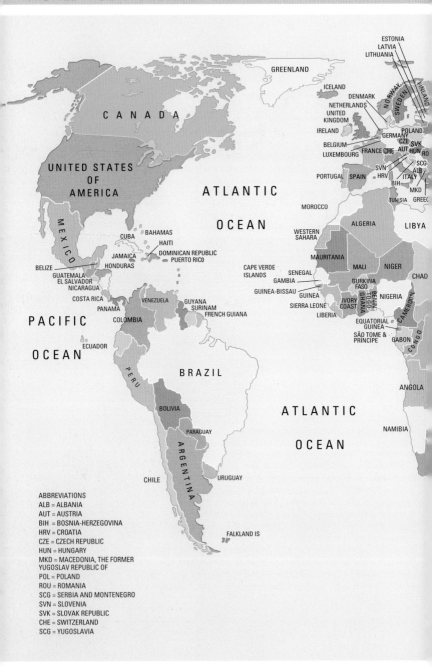

ESTONIA
LATVIA
LITHUANIA

GREENLAND

ICELAND

DENMARK
NETHERLANDS
UNITED
KINGDOM
IRELAND

NORWAY
SWEDEN
FINLAND

CANADA

POLAND
GERMANY
CZE SVK
BELGIUM
FRANCE CHE AUT HUN RO
LUXEMBOURG
SCG
SVN ALB
HRV ITALY
PORTUGAL SPAIN
BIH MKD
TUNISIA GREEC

UNITED STATES
OF
AMERICA

ATLANTIC

OCEAN

MOROCCO

MEXICO

CUBA BAHAMAS
HAITI
JAMAICA DOMINICAN REPUBLIC
HONDURAS PUERTO RICO
BELIZE
GUATEMALA
EL SALVADOR
NICARAGUA

WESTERN
SAHARA

ALGERIA

LIBYA

MAURITANIA

MALI NIGER

CHAD

CAPE VERDE
ISLANDS SENEGAL
GAMBIA
GUINEA-BISSAU GUINEA
SIERRA LEONE
LIBERIA

BURKINA
FASO
BENIN
IVORY TOGO NIGERIA
COAST GHANA

COSTA RICA
PANAMA

VENEZUELA GUYANA
SURINAM
COLOMBIA FRENCH GUIANA

EQUATORIAL
GUINEA
SÃO TOMÉ &
PRINCIPE GABON

CAMEROON

CONGO

PACIFIC

ECUADOR

OCEAN

PERU

BRAZIL

ANGOLA

ATLANTIC

BOLIVIA

PARAGUAY

NAMIBIA

OCEAN

ARGENTINA

CHILE URUGUAY

FALKLAND IS

ABBREVIATIONS
ALB = ALBANIA
AUT = AUSTRIA
BIH = BOSNIA-HERZEGOVINA
HRV = CROATIA
CZE = CZECH REPUBLIC
HUN = HUNGARY
MKD = MACEDONIA, THE FORMER
YUGOSLAV REPUBLIC OF
POL = POLAND
ROU = ROMANIA
SCG = SERBIA AND MONTENEGRO
SVN = SLOVENIA
SVK = SLOVAK REPUBLIC
CHE = SWITZERLAND
SCG = YUGOSLAVIA

BELARUS

RUSSIA

UKRAINE
MOLDOVA
BULGARIA GEORGIA
TURKEY
CYPRUS SYRIA
LEBANON
ISRAEL
JORDAN
EGYPT

KAZAKSTAN

ARMENIA AZER-
BAIJAN
UZBEKISTAN
TURKMENISTAN
TAJIKISTAN

KYRGYZSTAN

MONGOLIA

NORTH
KOREA

JAPAN

SOUTH
KOREA

PACIFIC

IRAQ IRAN
KUWAIT

SAUDI
ARABIA

AFGHAN-
ISTAN

NEPAL

PAKISTAN

BHUTAN

CHINA

TAIWAN

OCEAN

QATAR
UNITED
ARAB
EMIRATES

INDIA

BURMA

VIETNAM

SUDAN

ERITREA YEMEN OMAN

BANGLADESH

THAILAND

LAOS

CENTRAL
AFRICA

ETHIOPIA

DJIBOUTI

SRI
LANKA

CAMBODIA

PHILIPPINES

SOMALIA

UGANDA

KENYA

BRUNEI

MALAYSIA

CONGO
(DEM. REP.)

RWANDA
BURUNDI

SINGAPORE

TANZANIA

INDIAN OCEAN

INDONESIA

PAPUA
NEW
GUINEA

ZAMBIA

MALAWI

MOZAMBIQUE

ZIMBABWE

MADAGASCAR

BOTSWANA

AUSTRALIA

SWAZILAND

LESOTHO

SOUTH AFRICA

NEW
ZEALAND

Scale along the Equator

0   1000   2000   3000   4000 km

0   1000   2000 miles

ISO COUNTRY CODES

The country name codes used on the maps throughout this book, are the official codes used by the International Organization for Standardization. We have used the codes as stated in ISO 3166-1 alpha-3. The codes are listed here in alphabetical order.

A	
ABW	Aruba
AFG	Afghanistan
AGO	Angola
AIA	Anguilla
ALA	Åland Islands
ALB	Albania
AND	Andorra
ANT	Netherlands Antilles
ARE	United Arab Emirates
ARG	Argentina
ARM	Armenia
ASM	American Samoa
ATA	Antarctica
ATF	French Southern Territories
ATG	Antigua and Barbuda
AUS	Australia
AUT	Austria
AZE	Azerbaijan

B	
BDI	Burundi
BEL	Belgium
BEN	Benin
BFA	Burkina Faso
BGD	Bangladesh
BGR	Bulgaria
BHR	Bahrain
BHS	Bahamas
BIH	Bosnia-Herzegovina
BLR	Belarus
BLZ	Belize
BMU	Bermuda
BOL	Bolivia
BRA	Brazil
BRB	Barbados
BRN	Brunei
BTN	Bhutan
BVT	Bouvet Islands
BWA	Botswana

C	
CAF	Central African Republic
CAN	Canada
CCK	Cocos (Keeling) Islands
CHE	Switzerland
CHL	Chile
CHN	China
CIV	Ivory Coast
CMR	Cameroon
COD	Congo (Democratic Republic of)
COG	Congo
COK	Cook Islands
COL	Colombia
COM	Comoros
CPV	Cape Verde Islands
CRI	Costa Rica
CUB	Cuba
CXR	Christmas Island
CYM	Cayman Islands
CYP	Cyprus
CZE	Czech Republic

D	
DEU	Germany
DJI	Djibouti
DMA	Dominica
DNK	Denmark
DOM	Dominican Republic
DZA	Algeria

E	
ECU	Ecuador
EGY	Egypt
ERI	Eritrea
ESH	Western Sahara
ESP	Spain
EST	Estonia
ETH	Ethiopia

F	
FIN	Finland
FJI	Fiji
FLK	Falkland Islands
FRA	France
FRO	Faroe Islands
FSM	Micronesia, Federated States of

G	
GAB	Gabon
GBR	United Kingdom
GEO	Georgia
GHA	Ghana
GIB	Gibraltar
GIN	Guinea
GLP	Guadeloupe
GMB	Gambia, The
GNB	Guinea-Bissau
GNQ	Equatorial Guinea
GRC	Greece
GRD	Grenada
GRL	Greenland
GTM	Guatemala
GUF	French Guiana
GUM	Guam
GUY	Guyana

H	
HKG	Hong Kong
HMD	Heard Island and McDonald Islands
HND	Honduras
HRV	Croatia
HTI	Haiti
HUN	Hungary

I, J	
IDN	Indonesia
IND	India
IOT	British Indian Ocean Territory
IRL	Ireland
IRN	Iran
IRQ	Iraq
ISL	Iceland
ISR	Israel
ITA	Italy
JAM	Jamaica
JOR	Jordan
JPN	Japan

K	
KAZ	Kazakhstan
KEN	Kenya
KGZ	Kyrgyzstan
KHM	Cambodia
KIR	Kiribati
KNA	St Kitts and Nevis
KOR	Korea, South
KWT	Kuwait

L

LAO	Laos
LBN	Lebanon
LBR	Liberia
LBY	Libya
LCA	St Lucia
LIE	Liechtenstein
LKA	Sri Lanka
LSO	Lesotho
LTU	Lithuania
LUX	Luxembourg
LVA	Latvia

M

MAC	Macau
MAR	Morocco
MCO	Monaco
MDA	Moldova
MDG	Madagascar
MDV	Maldives
MEX	Mexico
MHL	Marshall Islands
MKD	Macedonia, The Former Yugoslav Republic of
MLI	Mali
MLT	Malta
MMR	Burma (Myanmar)
MNG	Mongolia
MNP	Northern Mariana Islands
MOZ	Mozambique
MRT	Mauritania
MSR	Montserrat
MTQ	Martinique
MUS	Mauritius
MWI	Malawi
MYS	Malaysia
MYT	Mayotte

N

NAM	Namibia
NCL	New Caledonia
NER	Niger
NFK	Norfolk Island
NGA	Nigeria
NIC	Nicaragua
NIU	Niue
NLD	Netherlands
NOR	Norway
NPL	Nepal
NRU	Nauru
NZL	New Zealand

O, P

OMN	Oman
PAK	Pakistan
PAN	Panama
PCN	Pitcairn Island
PER	Peru
PHL	Philippines
PLW	Palau
PNG	Papua New Guinea
POL	Poland
PRI	Puerto Rico
PRK	Korea, North
PRT	Portugal
PRY	Paraguay
PSE	West Bank
PYF	French Polynesia

Q, R

QAT	Qatar
REU	Réunion
ROU	Romania
RUS	Russia
RWA	Rwanda

S

SAU	Saudi Arabia
SCG	Serbia and Montenegro
SDN	Sudan
SEN	Senegal
SGP	Singapore
SGS	South Georgia and the South Sandwich Islands
SHN	St Helena
SJM	Svalbard
SLB	Solomon Islands
SLE	Sierra Leone
SLV	El Salvador
SMR	San Marino
SOM	Somalia
SPM	St Pierre and Miquelon
STP	São Tomé and Príncipe
SUR	Suriname
SVK	Slovak Republic
SVN	Slovenia
SWE	Sweden
SWZ	Swaziland
SYC	Seychelles
SYR	Syria

T

TCA	Turks and Caicos Islands
TCD	Chad
TGO	Togo
THA	Thailand
TJK	Tajikistan
TKL	Tokelau Islands
TKM	Turkmenistan
TLS	East Timor
TON	Tonga
TTO	Trinidad and Tobago
TUN	Tunisia
TUR	Turkey
TUV	Tuvalu
TWN	Taiwan
TZA	Tanzania

U

UGA	Uganda
UKR	Ukraine
UMI	United States Minor Outlying Islands
URY	Uruguay
USA	United States of America
UZB	Uzbekistan

V

VAT	Vatican City
VCT	St Vincent and the Grenadines
VEN	Venezuela
VGB	Virgin Islands (UK)
VIR	Virgin Islands (US)
VNM	Vietnam
VUT	Vanuatu

W, Y, Z

WLF	Wallis and Futuna Islands
WSM	Samoa
YEM	Yemen
ZAF	South Africa
ZMB	Zambia
ZWE	Zimbabwe

See the **Country Data** section (p194–203) for an alphabetical list of codes sorted by full country name. Only those countries with full statistical data are listed.

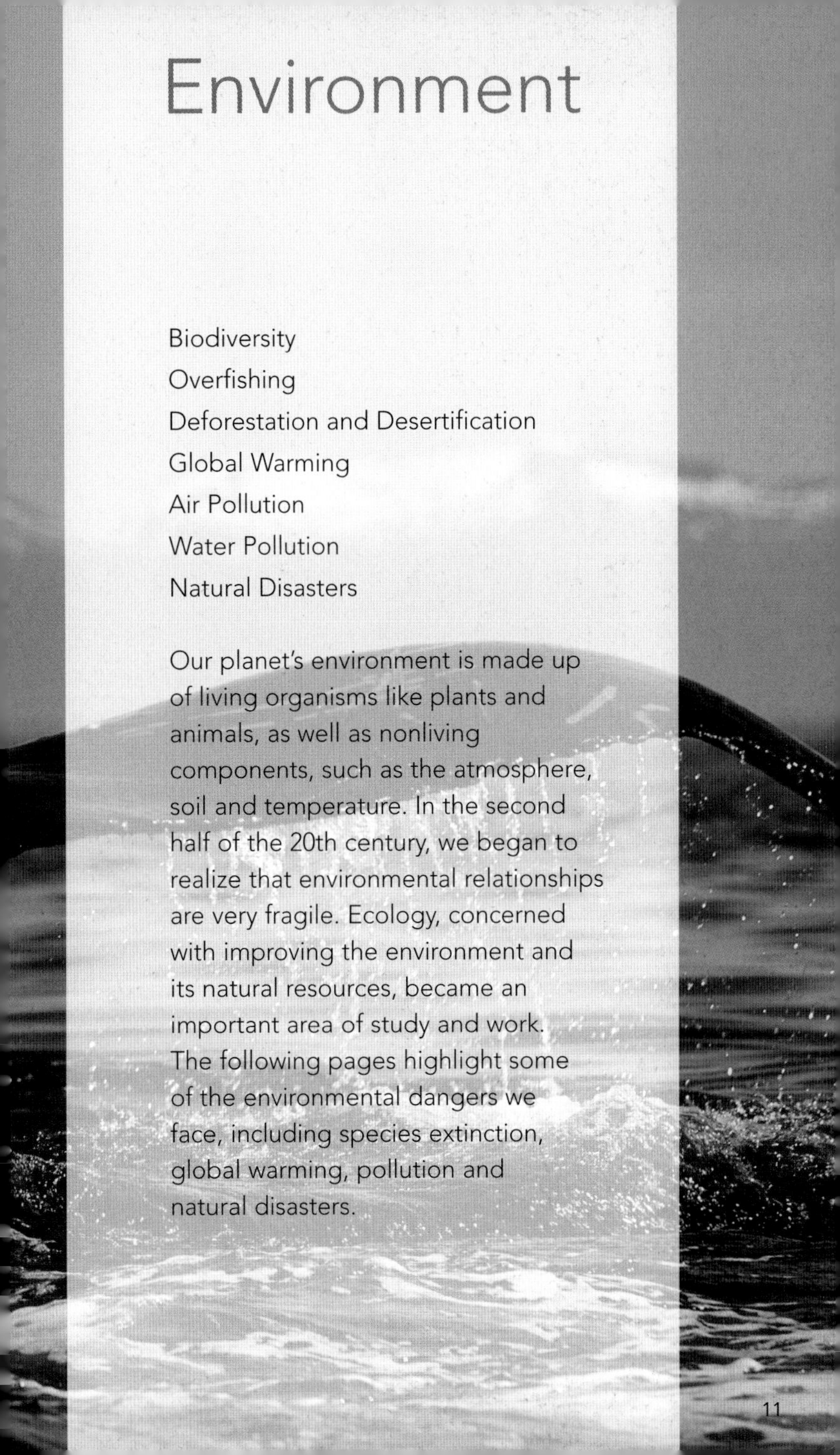

Environment

Biodiversity

Overfishing

Deforestation and Desertification

Global Warming

Air Pollution

Water Pollution

Natural Disasters

Our planet's environment is made up of living organisms like plants and animals, as well as nonliving components, such as the atmosphere, soil and temperature. In the second half of the 20th century, we began to realize that environmental relationships are very fragile. Ecology, concerned with improving the environment and its natural resources, became an important area of study and work. The following pages highlight some of the environmental dangers we face, including species extinction, global warming, pollution and natural disasters.

THREATENED SPECIES
Number of species on IUCN Red List per country

- Over 50
- 25–50
- 10–25
- 5–10
- Under 5
- No data

The map shows the number of threatened species in countries according to the International Union for Conservation of Nature and Natural Resources (IUCN). The biodiversity of plants and animals is of vital importance in balancing the environment. Scientists estimate that 100 species will become extinct every day throughout the 21st century. This is due to changes in the environment which are natural or caused by humans. Population growth, large-scale farming, hunting, fishing industrialization and pollution all affect biodiversity. Some species suffer when new ones are introduced into their territory; in Britain, the arrival of the larger, more aggressive American gray squirrel has endangered the native red one. Campaigns by governments and environmental groups are saving many species. Alligators in the US state of Louisiana, for example, have been taken off the endangered list after a ban on hunting restored their numbers. The international community also works together under the Convention of Biological Diversity (1992). However, there is still a need for greater awareness, campaigns, and effort to save more species from extinction.

See pages 8 and 9 for country abbreviations

NATIONAL BIODIVERSITY INDEX			
Most diverse (Top Ten)		**Least diverse* (Bottom Ten)**	
Indonesia	1.000	Iceland	0.113
Colombia	0.935	Qatar	0.189
Mexico	0.928	Kuwait	0.224
Brazil	0.877	Libya	0.240
Ecuador	0.873	Ireland	0.279
Australia	0.853	Saudi Arabia	0.281
Venezuela	0.850	Finland	0.290
Peru	0.843	Norway	0.297
China	0.839	Canada	0.299
Costa Rica	0.820	Sweden	0.304

◄ This index is based on estimates of country richness and endemism in four terrestrial vertebrate classes and vascular plants; vertebrates and plants are ranked equally; index values range between 1.000 (maximum: Indonesia) and 0.000 (minimum: Greenland, not shown in table).

*The NBI includes some adjustment allowing for country size. Countries with land area less than 5,000 sq km are excluded. Overseas territories and dependencies are excluded from this column.

13

BIODIVERSITY

The distribution of threatened birds is shown on this world map. Birds are very sensitive to any changes in their normal environment, and it is surprising how quickly a common species can become endangered. The English house sparrow, *Passer domesticus*, once dominated rural areas of Great Britain, but is seldom seen today because of modern farming techniques. Indeed, birds lead the threatened species list below on the Red List compiled by the International Union for Conservation of Nature and Natural Resources (IUCN). The table on the following page indicates that almost 10,000 plants are also endangered.

THREATENED SPECIES

Legend:
- 2002 Red list
- 1996 Red List

Species	2002 Red list	1996 Red List
Birds	1,192	1,107
Mammals	1,137	1,096
Molluscs	939	920
Fishes	742	734
Insects	557	537
Crustaceans	409	407
Reptiles	293	253
Amphibians	157	124

Map labels: GREENLAND, CANADA, USA, MEXICO, ATLANTIC OCEAN, PACIFIC OCEAN, CUB, BHS, HTI, DOM, PUERTO RICO, JAM, BLZ, GTM, HND, SLV, NIC, CRI, PAN, VEN, GUY, SUR, GUF, COL, ECU, BRAZIL, PERU, BOL, PRY, ARGENTINA, URY, CHL, FLK

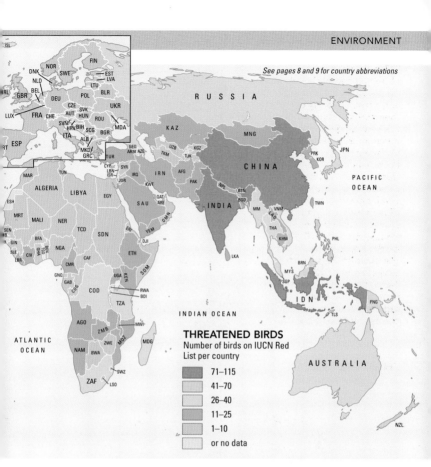

See pages 8 and 9 for country abbreviations

THREATENED BIRDS
Number of birds on IUCN Red
List per country

- 71–115
- 41–70
- 26–40
- 11–25
- 1–10
- or no data

THREATENED AND EXTINCT PLANTS		
Class	Extinct	Endangered
Magnoliopsida (dicotyledons)	74	7,734
Liliopsida (monocotyledons)	2	792
Coniferopsida (conifers)	0	618
Cycadopsida (cycads)	0	288
Polypodiopsida (true ferns)	2	164
Marchantiopsida (liverworts)	1	52
Bryopsida (true mosses)	2	39
Lycopodiopsida (club mosses)	0	13
Anthocerotopsida (hornworts)	0	2
Sellaginellopsida (spike mosses)	0	2
Isoetopsida (quillworts)	0	1
Ginkgopsida (gingkos)	0	1
Total	**81**	**9,706**

OVERFISHING

Fish caught in five major ocean areas are shown in the charts on this and the next page. Overfishing has caused the destruction of stocks worldwide, and 750 species were threatened in 2003. The greatest depletion has occurred in the Atlantic. Canadian officials say overfishing increased by 300% in 2003 and that rate will eliminate cod and American plaice within three to five years. The European Union also recorded record low stocks of cod. Although the Indian and Pacific oceans are the only oceans to have experienced a steady increase in production over the past 50 years, these oceans are now fully exploited.

In addition to the environmental impact of declining numbers of fish, overfishing also endangers the jobs of those whose livelihood depends on fishing. The graphic below indicates how the Atlantic cod catch of various countries has fallen from 1971 to 2001 due to falling stocks.

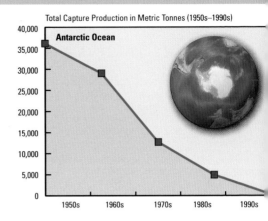

Total Capture Production in Metric Tonnes (1950s–1990s)

Antarctic Ocean

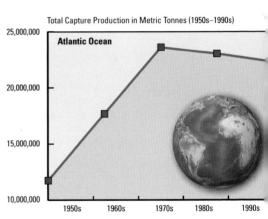

Total Capture Production in Metric Tonnes (1950s–1990s)

Atlantic Ocean

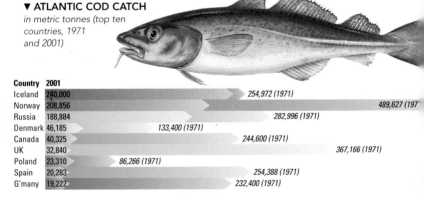

▼ **ATLANTIC COD CATCH**
in metric tonnes (top ten countries, 1971 and 2001)

Country	2001	1971
Iceland	240,000	254,972 (1971)
Norway	208,856	489,627 (197
Russia	188,884	282,996 (1971)
Denmark	46,185	133,400 (1971)
Canada	40,325	244,600 (1971)
UK	32,840	367,166 (1971)
Poland	23,310	86,266 (1971)
Spain	20,283	254,388 (1971)
G'many	19,222	232,400 (1971)

ENVIRONMENTAL IMPACT LEVELS: SEAFOOD

Good levels/little impact

Farmed mussels and clams
Alaska salmon
Crawfish
Alaska halibut
Dungeness crab
Catfish
Striped bass
Mahimahi
Pacific cod

Depleted/limited environmental impact

Pacific flounders/soles
Rainbow trout
Maine lobster
Squid
Yellowfin, bigeye and albacore tuna
Swordfish
Atlantic cod
Grouper
Shrimp
Atlantic flounders/soles
Monkfish
Shark
Bluefin tuna

Overfished/environmentally unsound

Farmed and Atlantic salmon
Orange roughy
Red snapper
Chilean seabass
Haddock
Skate
Atlantic halibut

▲ *Listed above are stock levels of seafood, with the most endangered types shown in the red zone. Farmed mussels, clams and salmon are included.*

Total Capture Production in Metric Tonnes (1950s–1990s)

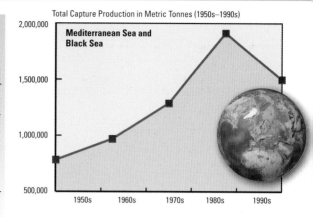

Total Capture Production in Metric Tonnes (1950s–1990s)

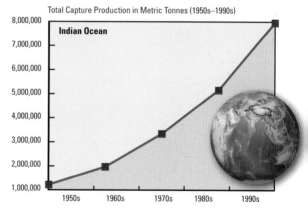

Total Capture Production in Metric Tonnes (1950s–1990s)

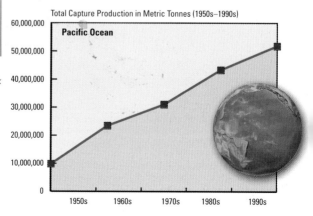

17

DESERTIFICATION AND DEFORESTATION

- Existing deserts
- Areas with a high risk of desertification
- Areas with a moderate risk of desertification
- Former areas of rain forest
- Existing rain forest

This map indicates the regions of the world where rain forests are being reduced and deserts are expanding. Deforestation is implemented by humans when they need to clear land for agriculture, timber or building sites. Vital topsoil is then eroded by wind and rain. Clearing immense areas, such as the Brazilian rain forest, can cause an environmental catastrophe by upsetting the Earth's oxygen balance. Every month, an estimated 1.1 hectares (2.8 million acres) of the world's tropical forests are lost.

The removal of vegetation, by people, overgrazing, or the climate, can also cause desertification with sand expanding over adjacent fertile land. Desertlike conditions threaten a third of the Earth, or more than 4 billion hectares (10 billion acres). The United Nations holds an annual World Day to Combat Desertification and Drought on June 17.

LARGEST DESERTS			
Desert	Country/Region	Sq km	Sq mi
Sahara	Africa	8,600,000	3,320,000
Arabian	Asia	2,230,000	900,000
Gobi	Mongolia, China	1,166,000	450,000
Patagonian	Argentina	673,000	260,000
Great Victoria	Australia	647,000	250,000
Great Basin	USA	492,000	190,000
Chihuahua	Mexico	450,000	175,000
Great Sandy	Australia	400,000	150,000
Sonora	USA	310,000	120,000
Kyzyl Kum	Kazakstan	300,000	115,000
Takla Makan	China	270,000	105,000
Kalahari	Africa	260,000	100,000
Kara Kum	Turkmenistan	260,000	100,000
Kavir	Iran	260,000	100,000
Syrian	Middle East	260,000	100,000

▼ *These Landsat images* from 1975 to 2000 show the deforestation (left to right) of an area of tropical dry forest to the east of the city of Santa Cruz, eastern Bolivia. Since the mid 1980s, a large agricultural development effort (the Tierras Baja project) and the San Javier scheme for the resettlement of people from the Altiplano (the Andean high plains) has lead to this area's deforestation. The light colored areas are fields of soybeans.

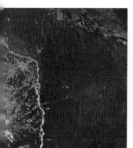

19

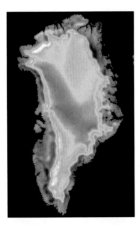

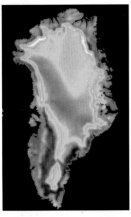

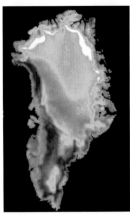

The world map shows the average amount of carbon dioxide (CO_2) produced in each country per person. Such emissions lead to the greenhouse effect when heat energy is trapped by gases in the atmosphere, raising temperatures and producing global warming. Some scientists blame the effects of global warming for increasingly erratic weather patterns. As the map indicates, the industrialized nations create most greenhouse gas emissions. The average American creates 17.5 metric tonnes of carbon dioxide, while an Ethiopian produces only 100 kg (220 lbs). In 1997, the Kyoto Protocol was framed by more than 160 nations meeting in Kyoto, Japan, to cut emissions linked to global warming. It remains unratified because the USA and Russia have not signed. The three NASA images to the left show the Greenland ice sheets melting at five-day intervals. Red and black areas indicate melting snow. This process releases freshwater into the ocean. A rise of just 4°C (7°F) is considered enough to cause the complete melting of the Greenland Icecap.

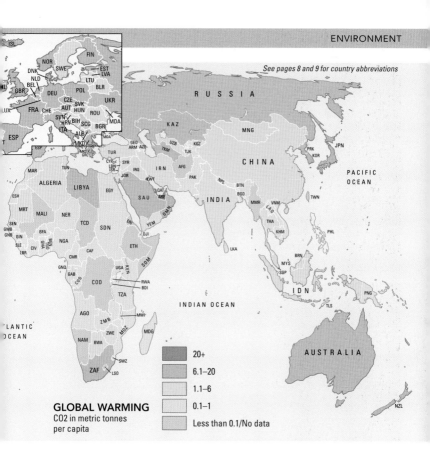

See pages 8 and 9 for country abbreviations

GLOBAL WARMING
CO2 in metric tonnes
per capita

	20+
	6.1–20
	1.1–6
	0.1–1
	Less than 0.1/No data

▼ *Projected change in global warming*
Even if countries make immediate drastic cuts in greenhouse gas emissions, global temperatures are still predicted to rise 2.5°C (5°F) by the year 2050.

Rise in average temperatures assuming present trends in CO₂ emissions continue

Assuming some cuts are made in emissions

Assuming drastic cuts are made in emissions

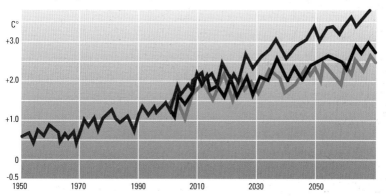

AIR POLLUTION

The map below shows that air pollution is a problem in both developing and industrialized nations. Although great improvements have been made in the West, the American Lung Association said in 2004 that more than 159 million Americans are breathing unhealthy levels of ozone or particle pollution. Smog, a mixture of smoke and fog or chemical fumes, remains an issue and can cause numerous health problems. In 1955, a five-day smog in London took c.4,000 lives. Air pollution also affects the Earth's ozone layer that protects against harmful ultraviolet radiation. The layer is being broken down by fumes and the chlorofluorocarbons (CFCs) used in fire extinguishers, refrigerants and aerosols.

THE MOST POLLUTED CITIES

TOTAL SUSPENDED PARTICLES		
Micrograms per cubic meter		
Lanzhou	China	732
Taiyuan	China	568
Urumqi	China	515
Zhengzhou	China	474
Jinan	China	472
Lucknow	India	463
Kanpur	India	459
Zibo	China	453
Delhi	India	415
Liupanshui	China	408

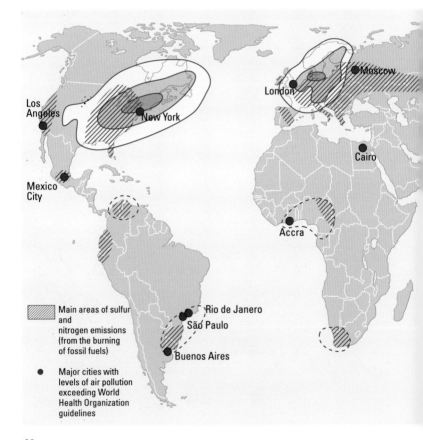

Main areas of sulfur and nitrogen emissions (from the burning of fossil fuels)

● Major cities with levels of air pollution exceeding World Health Organization guidelines

SULFUR DIOXIDE		
Micrograms per cubic meter		
Guiyang	China	424
Chongqing	China	340
Taiyuan	China	211
Tehran	Iran	209
Zibo	China	198
Quingdao	China	190
Jinan	China	132
Rio de Janeiro	Brazil	129
Ankara	Turkey	120
Anshan	China	115

NITROGEN DIOXIDE		
Micrograms per cubic meter		
Milan	Italy	248
Guangzhu	China	136
Mexico City	Mexico	130
Sofia	Bulgaria	122
Beijing	China	122
Lanzhou	China	104
Dalian	China	100
Córdoba City	Argentina	97
Zhengzhou	China	95
Anshan	China	88

◄ *These three lists of the world's most polluted cities are dominated by China and other developing countries. Suspended particles and sulfur dioxide can cause lung and heart disease, while nitrogen dioxide may cause respiratory infections.*

▼ **Atmospheric ozone concentration** with the hole of the ozone layer in the center.

AIR POLLUTION

- pH 4.5–5.0
- pH 4.0–4.5
- pH less than 4.0 (most acidic)
- Potential problem areas

Northern hemisphere (March 2000)

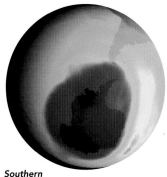

Southern hemisphere (September 2000)

WATER POLLUTION

TOP TEN OIL TANKER DISASTERS

	Tanker name	Tonnes spilled	Year
1	Atlantic Express	287,000	1979
2	ABT Summer	260,000	1991
3	Castillo de Bellver	252,000	1983
4	Amoco Cadiz	223,000	1978
5	Haven	144,000	1991
6	Odyssey	132,000	1988
7	Torrey Canyon	119,000	1967
8	Urquiola	100,000	1976
9	Hawaiian Patriot	95,000	1977
10	Independenta	95,000	1979

WATER POLLUTION

- ⬛ Severely polluted sea areas and lakes
- ◼ Less polluted sea areas and lakes
- ◻ Areas of frequent oil pollution by shipping
- ⑨ ◯ Major oil tanker spills
- ▲ Major oil rig blow-outs
- ▼ Offshore dumpsites for industrial and municipal waste
- — Severely polluted rivers and estuaries

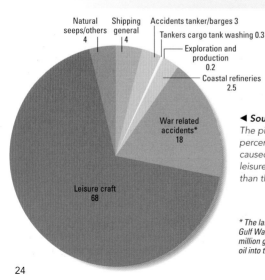

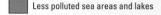

Natural seeps/others 4 | Shipping general 4 | Accidents tanker/barges 3
Tankers cargo tank washing 0.3
Exploration and production 0.2
Coastal refineries 2.5
War related accidents* 18
Leisure craft 68

◀ **Sources of water pollution**
The pie chart indicates the percentages of water pollution caused by major sources. Small leisure craft cause far more problems than the spectacular oil tanker spills.

* The largest oil spill occurred during the 1991 Gulf War when Iraq deliberately released c.240 million gallons (about 800,000 tonnes) of crude oil into the Persian Gulf.

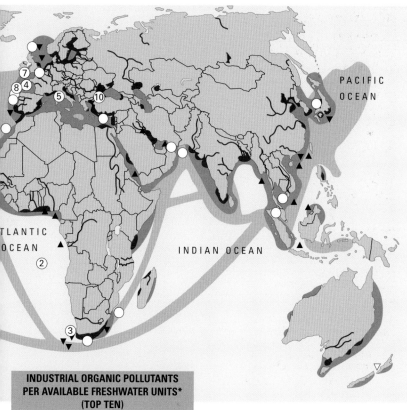

INDUSTRIAL ORGANIC POLLUTANTS PER AVAILABLE FRESHWATER UNITS* (TOP TEN)

1	Israel	27.1
2	Jordan	11.5
3	Tunisia	11.4
4	Algeria	8.6
5	Czech Republic	7.9
6	Morocco	7.9
7	Denmark	7.1
8	Poland	5.9
9	Korea, South	5.7
10	Ukraine	5.5

*Metric tons of BOD (biochemical oxygen demands) per cubic km of water. The BOD is the amount of oxygen that bacteria in water will consume in breaking down waste. This is a standard water-treatment test for the presence of organic pollutants.

The world map shows the 10 largest oil spills by tankers, but this is not the same as ecological damage. The *Exxon Valdez*, for instance, spilled 38,800 tonnes in Alaskan waters in 1989. This is not even in the top 50 by volume, but it is considered the worst environmental disaster, with oil on some 2,090 km (1,300 mi) of the shoreline and extensive damage to wildlife. Water pollution also causes danger closer to home. Rivers and lakes may suffer because a nearby industry releases chemicals, waste or sewage. Farms also pollute waterways by the runoff of fertilizers and organic waste products. The average household cleaning products are pollutants, as are domestic pesticides and herbicides. Acid rain, landslides and silt can also pollute.

25

NATURAL DISASTERS

Pinpointed on this map are the locations of major natural disasters during the last quarter-century. Weather and land occurrences, often violent, have caused deaths, injuries, disease, hunger and physical damage. Six of the 13 worst natural disasters of the 20th century listed below involve diseases. Nature's most violent moments throughout history have come from volcanoes, earthquakes, floods and hurricanes. Tragic examples include the Vesuvius eruption that destroyed Pompeii in AD 79, the earthquake that devastated San Francisco in 1906, the Huang He River flood in China that killed 3.7 million people in 1931 and the hurricane that caused more than 8,000 deaths in Galveston, Texas in 1900. Despite the natural cause of the event itself, economic factors affect the impact of the disaster. According to the World Bank, 96% of disaster-related deaths in 1999 occurred in developing countries. Poorer countries are less able to prepare for a disaster, and less able to provide relief following a disaster.

⊗ Landslide/avalanche
≈ Flood
🔥 Fire
Drought
⚡ Wind storm
▲ Volcano
▦ Earthquake
● Epidemic

THE WORST NATURAL DISASTERS OF THE 20TH CENTURY				
Country	Location	Disaster type	Date	Killed
–	Worldwide	Influenza epidemic	1917	20,000,000
Soviet Union	Nationwide	Famine	1932	5,000,000
China	–	Flood	July 1931	3,700,000
Serbia, Poland, Russia	–	Typhus epidemic	July 1914	3,000,000
China	Shaanxi, Henan, Gansu	Drought	1928	3,000,000
Russia	Nationwide	unknown epidemic	1917	2,500,000
China	–	Flood	July 1959	2,000,000
India	–	Bubonic Plague	1920	2,000,000
Bangladesh	–	Famine	1943	1,900,000
China	–	Bubonic Plague	1909	1,500,000
India	Calcutta, Bengal	Drought	1942	1,500,000
India	–	Drought	1965–67	1,500,000
India	–	Bubonic Plague	1907	1,300,000

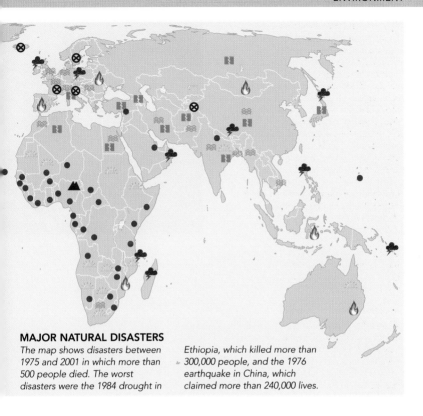

MAJOR NATURAL DISASTERS

The map shows disasters between 1975 and 2001 in which more than 500 people died. The worst disasters were the 1984 drought in Ethiopia, which killed more than 300,000 people, and the 1976 earthquake in China, which claimed more than 240,000 lives.

AVERAGE ANNUAL DAMAGES

Estimated damages (US$ million) per disaster type

30,000 —
25,000 —
20,000 —
15,000 —
10,000 —
5,000 —

Africa   Americas   Asia   Europe   Oceania

Proportion of damages per disaster type

0.8 —
0.6 —
0.4 —
0.2 —
0 —

Africa   Americas   Asia   Europe   Oceania

◀ **Average annual damages** (in US dollars) in disasters occurring between 1990 and 2001, and proportion of damages per disaster type.

Other
Wind storm
Volcano
Flood
Earthquake
Drought
Avalanche/ Landslide

27

NATURAL DISASTERS

The composite visual here shows a hurricane progressing from the Caribbean past Florida and Cuba into the Gulf of Mexico before it makes landfall between Louisiana and Texas. Hurricanes are easy to track by satellites and special aircraft that can even fly into the peaceful 'eye' of the storm. They are unpredictable, however, and residents of many cities and towns may be forced to evacuate before one comes ashore. Some in the US head north up the eastern shoreline. Hurricanes were once named only for women, but now alternate between the sexes, such as Alex, Bonnie, Charley and Danielle in 2004.

A hurricane's spiraling winds can reach more than 320km/h (200mph) and affect millions of people, as shown on the list of worst hurricanes. A cyclonic storm in the Pacific Ocean is called a typhoon.

▼ *The sketches below are sized to represent the different numbers of deaths in major volcanic eruptions. The most deadly eruption on the Caribbean island of Martinique totally destroyed the original capital of St. Pierre.*

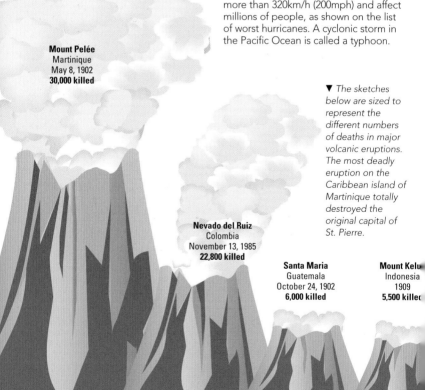

Mount Pelée
Martinique
May 8, 1902
30,000 killed

Nevado del Ruiz
Colombia
November 13, 1985
22,800 killed

Santa Maria
Guatemala
October 24, 1902
6,000 killed

Mount Kelu
Indonesia
1909
5,500 killed

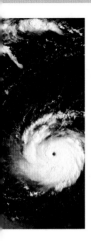

WORST HURRICANES (1975–2001)				
Location	Date	Name	People killed*	People affected
Bangladesh	March 30, 1991	Brendan	138,866	15,000,000
Central America	October 26, 1998	Mitch	18,599	3,240,200
India	November 12, 1977	–	14,204	9,037,400
Bangladesh	May 25, 1985	–	10,000	1,300,000
India	October 29, 1999	05B	9,843	12,625,000
Philippines	November 5, 1991	Thelma (Uring)	5,956	598,454
Vietnam	November 2, 1997	Linda	3,682	697,225
India	June 9, 1998	–	2,871	4,600,000
Caribbean	August 1979	David and Frederick	1,440	1,270,000
Southeast Asia	September 1984	Ike	1,412	1,237,224

People killed directly by hurricane

▼ Listed below are the world's major earthquakes by loss of life. Hardest hit have been the developing countries where, due to poverty, most buildings are unsafely constructed. The Richter scale measures the energy released by an earthquake, but the largest are not always the deadliest. The highest number ever recorded was 9.5 in southern Chile in 1960 when c.5,000 people died.

MAJOR EARTHQUAKES (1970–2003)					
Location(s)	Country	Richter scale	Date	Killed	Affected
Tangshan, Beijing, Tianjin	China	7.8	July 27, 1976	242,000	–
Bam	Iran	6.3	December 26, 2003	40,000	–
Gilan, Zanjan provinces	Iran	7.3	June 1, 1990	40,000	605,000
Leninakan, Kirovakan, Spitak	Armenia	6.9	December 7, 1988	25,000	1,642,000
Guatemala City	Guatemala	7.5	February 4, 1976	23,000	4,993,000
Gujarat state	India	7.9	January 26, 2001	20,005	16,066,812
Khorasan province	Iran	7.7	September 16, 1978	20,000	40,000
Izmit	Turkey	7.4	August 17, 1999	17,127	1,358,953
Maharastra state	India	6.4	September 23, 1993	9,782	195,566
Mexico City, Michoacán, Jalisco	Mexico	8.1	September 19, 1985	8,776	130,204

Mount Kelud
Indonesia
May 1919
5,000 killed

Santiaguito
Guatemala
1929
5,000 killed

Mount Lamington
Papua New Guinea
January 15, 1951
3,000 killed

Nyos
Cameroon
August 21, 1986
1,746 killed

Mount Agung
Indonesia
January 3, 1963
1,584 killed

Mount Soufrière
St Vincent & Grenadines
May 7, 1902
1,565 killed

Population

A keen understanding of a nation's population is crucial to its government's plans for the future. Populations have been measured since ancient times, with censuses mentioned in the Old Testament. The information in modern censuses is used to help formulate such government policies as economic development and social issues.
On a much broader scale, the current explosion in the world's population is a harbinger of future problems now being addressed by international bodies.

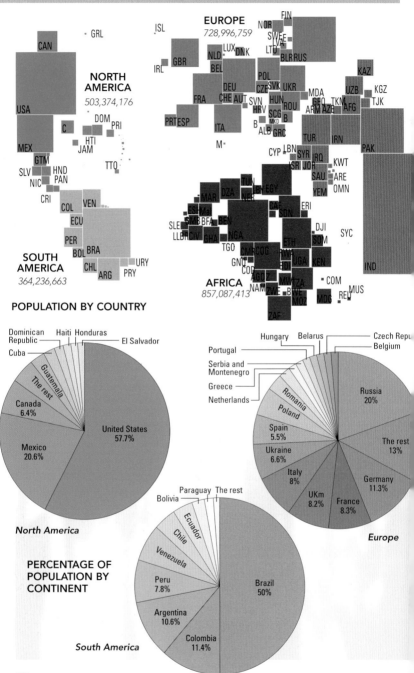

EUROPE
728,996,759

NORTH AMERICA
503,374,176

SOUTH AMERICA
364,236,663

AFRICA
857,087,413

POPULATION BY COUNTRY

North America pie chart:
- United States 57.7%
- Mexico 20.6%
- Canada 6.4%
- The rest
- Guatemala
- Cuba
- Dominican Republic
- Haiti
- Honduras
- El Salvador

North America

Europe pie chart:
- Russia 20%
- The rest 13%
- Germany 11.3%
- France 8.3%
- UKm 8.2%
- Italy 8%
- Ukraine 6.6%
- Spain 5.5%
- Poland
- Romania
- Netherlands
- Greece
- Serbia and Montenegro
- Portugal
- Hungary
- Belarus
- Czech Repu
- Belgium

Europe

South America pie chart:
- Brazil 50%
- Colombia 11.4%
- Argentina 10.6%
- Peru 7.8%
- Venezuela
- Chile
- Ecuador
- Bolivia
- Paraguay
- The rest

PERCENTAGE OF POPULATION BY CONTINENT

South America

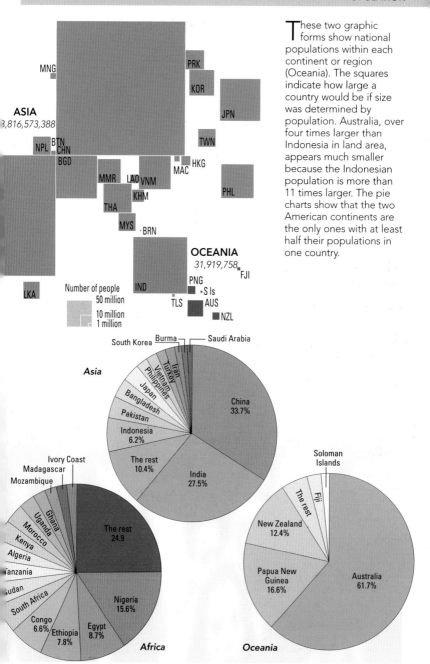

The two graphic forms show national populations within each continent or region (Oceania). The squares indicate how large a country would be if size was determined by population. Australia, over four times larger than Indonesia in land area, appears much smaller because the Indonesian population is more than 11 times larger. The pie charts show that the two American continents are the only ones with at least half their populations in one country.

ASIA
3,816,573,388

MNG
PRK
KOR
JPN
TWN
NPL BTN CHN
BGD
HKG
MAC
MMR LAO VNM
KHM
THA
MYS · BRN
PHL
LKA
IND

OCEANIA
31,919,758 · FJI
PNG
· S Is
TLS AUS
NZL

Number of people
50 million
10 million
1 million

Asia

South Korea — Burma — Saudi Arabia
Iran
Turkey
Vietnam
Philippines
Japan
Bangladesh
Pakistan
Indonesia 6.2%
The rest 10.4%
China 33.7%
India 27.5%

Africa

Ivory Coast
Madagascar
Mozambique
Ghana
Uganda
Morocco
Kenya
Algeria
Tanzania
Sudan
South Africa
Congo 6.6%
Ethiopia 7.8%
Egypt 8.7%
Nigeria 15.6%
The rest 24.9

Oceania

Soloman Islands
Fiji
The rest
New Zealand 12.4%
Papua New Guinea 16.6%
Australia 61.7%

B ar graphs on these two pages show the percentages of men and women at certain age groups on the continents and Oceania. Figures are given for 2003 and projections for 2050. Below each year's name is the total population figure, with the projected population increase or decrease between 2003 and 2050. The statistics reveal that males first outnumber females in the populations of all regions, but this is reversed during the middle and later years. Surprising facts in the four boxes are that Qatar has almost twice the number of men as women, and that the majority of Uganda's population is under the age of 15.

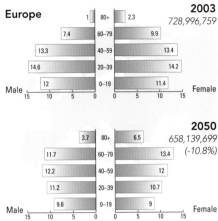

Europe

2003
728,996,759

Male	Age	Female
1	80+	2.3
7.4	60–79	9.9
13.3	40–59	13.4
14.6	20–39	14.2
12	0–19	11.4

2050
658,139,699
(-10.8%)

Male	Age	Female
3.7	80+	6.5
11.7	60–79	13.4
12.2	40–59	12
11.2	20–39	10.7
9.6	0–19	9

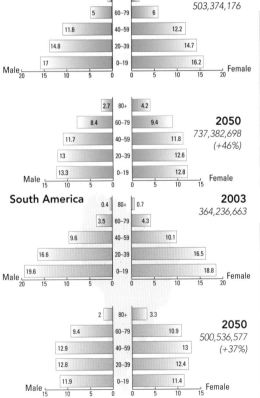

North America

2003
503,374,176

Male	Age	Female
0.9	80+	1.7
5	60–79	6
11.6	40–59	12.2
14.8	20–39	14.7
17	0–19	16.2

2050
737,382,698
(+46%)

Male	Age	Female
2.7	80+	4.2
8.4	60–79	9.4
11.7	40–59	11.8
13	20–39	12.6
13.3	0–19	12.8

South America

2003
364,236,663

Male	Age	Female
0.4	80+	0.7
3.5	60–79	4.3
9.6	40–59	10.1
16.6	20–39	16.5
19.6	0–19	18.8

2050
500,536,577
(+37%)

Male	Age	Female
2	80+	3.3
9.4	60–79	10.9
12.9	40–59	13
12.8	20–39	12.4
11.9	0–19	11.4

FEWEST MEN PER 100 WOMEN	
1 Latvia	84.3
2 Ukraine	86.8
3 Russia	88.0
4 Estonia	88.7
5. Belarus	88.0
6 Lithuania	89.7
7 Georgia	91.4
8 Hungary	91.6
= Moldova	91.6
10 Swaziland	92.4

PERCENTAGE OF PEOPLE AGED UNDER 15	
1 Uganda	50.8
2 Gaza Strip	49.4
3 Congo, Dem. Rep. of the	48.3
4 Chad	47.9
5 São Tomé and Principe	47.7
6 Niger	47.6
7 Mali	47.2
8 Benin	47.0
9 Malawi	46.8
10 Yemen	46.8

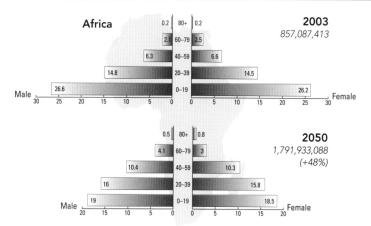

Africa

0.2	80+	0.2
2.1	60–79	2.5
6.3	40–59	6.6
14.8	20–39	14.5
26.6	0–19	26.2

Male 30 25 20 15 10 5 0 0 5 10 15 20 25 30 Female

2003
857,087,413

0.5	80+	0.8
4.1	60–79	3
10.4	40–59	10.3
16	20–39	15.8
19	0–19	18.5

Male 20 15 10 5 0 0 5 10 15 20 Female

2050
1,791,933,088
(+48%)

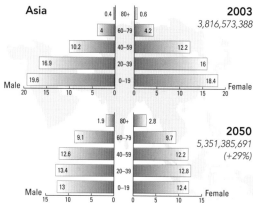

Asia

0.4	80+	0.6
4	60–79	4.2
10.2	40–59	12.2
16.9	20–39	16
19.6	0–19	18.4

Male 20 15 10 5 0 0 5 10 15 20 Female

2003
3,816,573,388

1.9	80+	2.8
9.1	60–79	9.7
12.6	40–59	12.2
13.4	20–39	12.8
13	0–19	12.4

Male 15 10 5 0 0 5 10 15 Female

2050
5,351,385,691
(+29%)

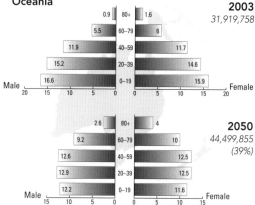

Oceania

0.9	80+	1.6
5.5	60–79	6
11.9	40–59	11.7
15.2	20–39	14.6
16.6	0–19	15.9

Male 20 15 10 5 0 0 5 10 15 20 Female

2003
31,919,758

2.6	80+	4
9.2	60–79	10
12.6	40–59	12.5
12.9	20–39	12.5
12.2	0–19	11.6

Male 15 10 5 0 0 5 10 15 Female

2050
44,499,855
(39%)

MOST MEN PER 100 WOMEN

1	Qatar	193.3
2	United Arab Emirates	176.4
3	Bahrain	133.7
4	Saudi Arabia	125.1
5	Oman	113.4
6	Trinidad and Tobago	111.3
7	Brunei	110.3
8	Tunisia	109.8
9	Libya	108.2
10	Hong Kong	107.6

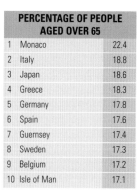

PERCENTAGE OF PEOPLE AGED OVER 65

1	Monaco	22.4
2	Italy	18.8
3	Japan	18.6
4	Greece	18.3
5	Germany	17.8
6	Spain	17.6
7	Guernsey	17.4
8	Sweden	17.3
9	Belgium	17.2
10	Isle of Man	17.1

35

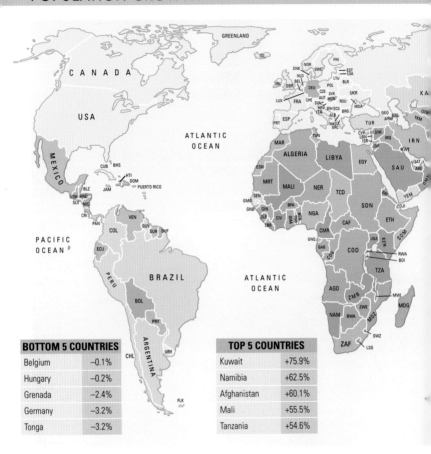

BOTTOM 5 COUNTRIES

Belgium	−0.1%
Hungary	−0.2%
Grenada	−2.4%
Germany	−3.2%
Tonga	−3.2%

TOP 5 COUNTRIES

Kuwait	+75.9%
Namibia	+62.5%
Afghanistan	+60.1%
Mali	+55.5%
Tanzania	+54.6%

POPULATION CHANGE 1930–2020

	1930	1930–1960	1960	1960–1990	1990	1990–2020	2020
World	2,013	1.4%	3,019	1.9%	5,292	1.4%	8,062
Africa	155	2.0%	281	2.9%	648	2.7%	1,441
North America	135	1.3%	199	1.1%	276	0.6%	327
South America*	129	1.8%	218	2.4%	448	1.6%	719
Asia	1,073	1.5%	1,669	2.1%	3,108	1.4%	4,680
Europe	355	0.6%	425	0.6%	498	0.1%	514
Australasia	10	1.4%	16	1.8%	27	1.1%	37
CIS†	176	0.7%	214	1.0%	288	0.6%	343

* South America plus Central America, Mexico and the West Indies
† Commonwealth of Independent States, formerly the USSR

◄ Population totals (left) are in millions, while figures in italics represent the percentage of average annual increase for the periods shown. The map shows how population growth in Western countries has slowed or even fallen. The graph (right) reveals the extraordinar

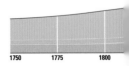

1750	1775	1800

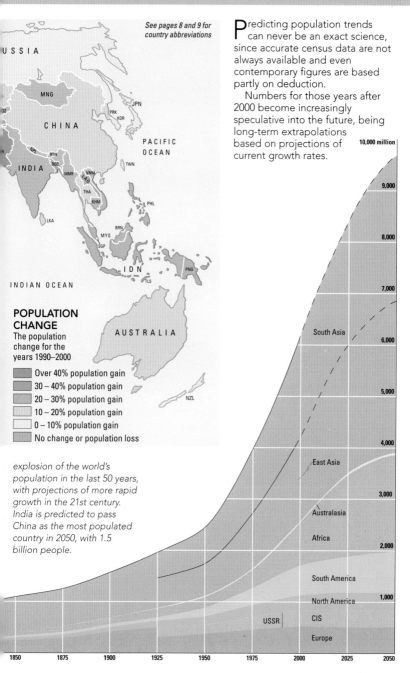

See pages 8 and 9 for country abbreviations

Predicting population trends can never be an exact science, since accurate census data are not always available and even contemporary figures are based partly on deduction.

Numbers for those years after 2000 become increasingly speculative into the future, being long-term extrapolations based on projections of current growth rates.

POPULATION CHANGE
The population change for the years 1990–2000

- Over 40% population gain
- 30 – 40% population gain
- 20 – 30% population gain
- 10 – 20% population gain
- 0 – 10% population gain
- No change or population loss

explosion of the world's population in the last 50 years, with projections of more rapid growth in the 21st century. India is predicted to pass China as the most populated country in 2050, with 1.5 billion people.

37

URBAN POPULATION

The main map shows the number of people living in urban areas as a percentage of the total country population (2000). Large countries such as Australia, the USA and Russia are still largely rural in nature and yet a shift in work trends over the past century has seen the majority of the population concentrated into smaller urban areas. Many countries in Africa are reliant on agriculture and still have a mainly rural population. The four smaller maps demonstrate the rapid appearance of cities since the 1850s. Urbanization continues at varying rates throughout the world. New York City, the world's largest city in 1950, reached a peak in 1970, but it has experienced periods of negative growth. London's population also declined between 1970 and 1985, before resuming a modest rate of increase. In both cases, the divergence from world trends is explained in part by counting methods. Each lies at the center of a great agglomeration, and definitions of the 'city limits' may vary over time. Rapid urban growth is now greatest, in some regions, in the smaller cities. For example, in Eastern India while Kolkata (Calcutta) remains the biggest city in terms of population, the population growth is higher in smaller cities.

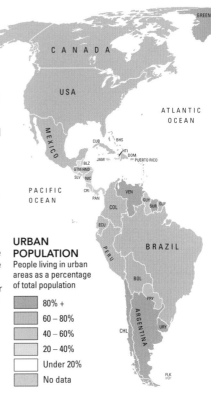

URBAN POPULATION
People living in urban areas as a percentage of total population

- 80% +
- 60 – 80%
- 40 – 60%
- 20 – 40%
- Under 20%
- No data

EXPANDING CITIES
The growth of some of the world's largest cities in millions, 1950–2015.

1950
2015

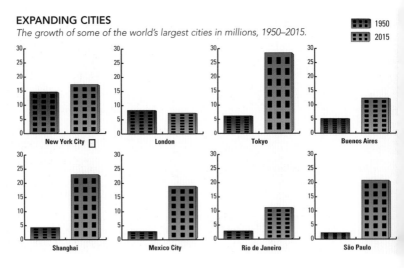

New York City

London

Tokyo

Buenos Aires

Shanghai

Mexico City

Rio de Janeiro

São Paulo

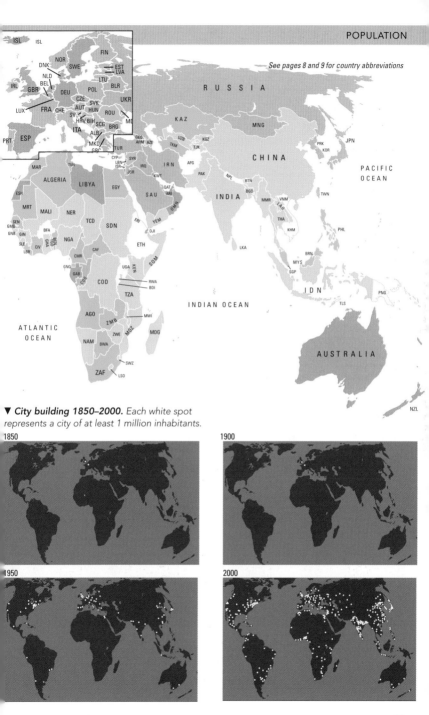

See pages 8 and 9 for country abbreviations

▼ **City building 1850–2000.** *Each white spot represents a city of at least 1 million inhabitants.*

1850

1900

1950

2000

POPULATION DENSITY

In 8000 BC, following the development of agriculture, the world had an estimated population of 8 million and by AD 1000 it was about 300 million. The onset of the Industrial Revolution in the late 18th century led to a population explosion. The 1,000 million mark was passed by 1850, it doubled by the 1920s, and doubled again to 4,000 million by 1975.

In the 1990s, UN demographers estimated that the world's population, which passed the 6 billion mark in 1999, would reach 8.9 billion by 2050 and only level out in 2200, at a peak of around 11 billion. However, in the early 21st century, after the rate of population growth had shown signs of decline, the Institute for Applied Systems Analysis (Laxenburg, Austria), suggested that the world's population might peak at about 9 billion in 2070. Whatever the global projections, everyone agreed that the greatest population growth will be in the developing countries.

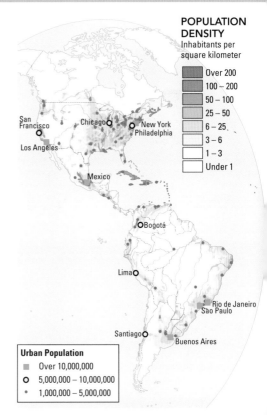

POPULATION DENSITY
Inhabitants per square kilometer

- Over 200
- 100 – 200
- 50 – 100
- 25 – 50
- 6 – 25
- 3 – 6
- 1 – 3
- Under 1

Urban Population
- ■ Over 10,000,000
- O 5,000,000 – 10,000,000
- · 1,000,000 – 5,000,000

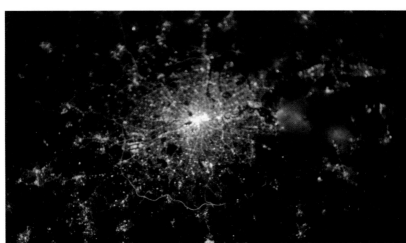

▼ **Projected largest cities**
Cities with more than 10 million inhabitants, based on estimates for the year 2015.

Early in the 21st century, for the first time in history, the majority of the world's population will live in cities.

◄ **London, Europe's largest city,** glimmers in this image taken from space in 2003. The population density in Westminster in the city's heart is now 7,539 per sq km.

LARGEST CITIES IN 2015 (MILLIONS)				
1.	Tokyo-Yokohama	28.7	11. Kolkata (Calcutta)	17.6
2.	Mumbai (Bombay)	27.4	12. Delhi	17.6
3.	Lagos	27.4	13. New York	17.6
4.	Shanghai	23.4	14. Tianjin	17.0
5.	Jakarta	21.2	15. Manila	14.7
6.	São Paulo	20.8	16. Cairo	14.5
7.	Karachi	20.6	17. Los Angeles	14.3
8.	Beijing	19.4	18. Seoul	13.1
9.	Dhaka	19.0	19. Buenos Aires	12.4
10.	Mexico City	18.8	20. Istanbul	12.3

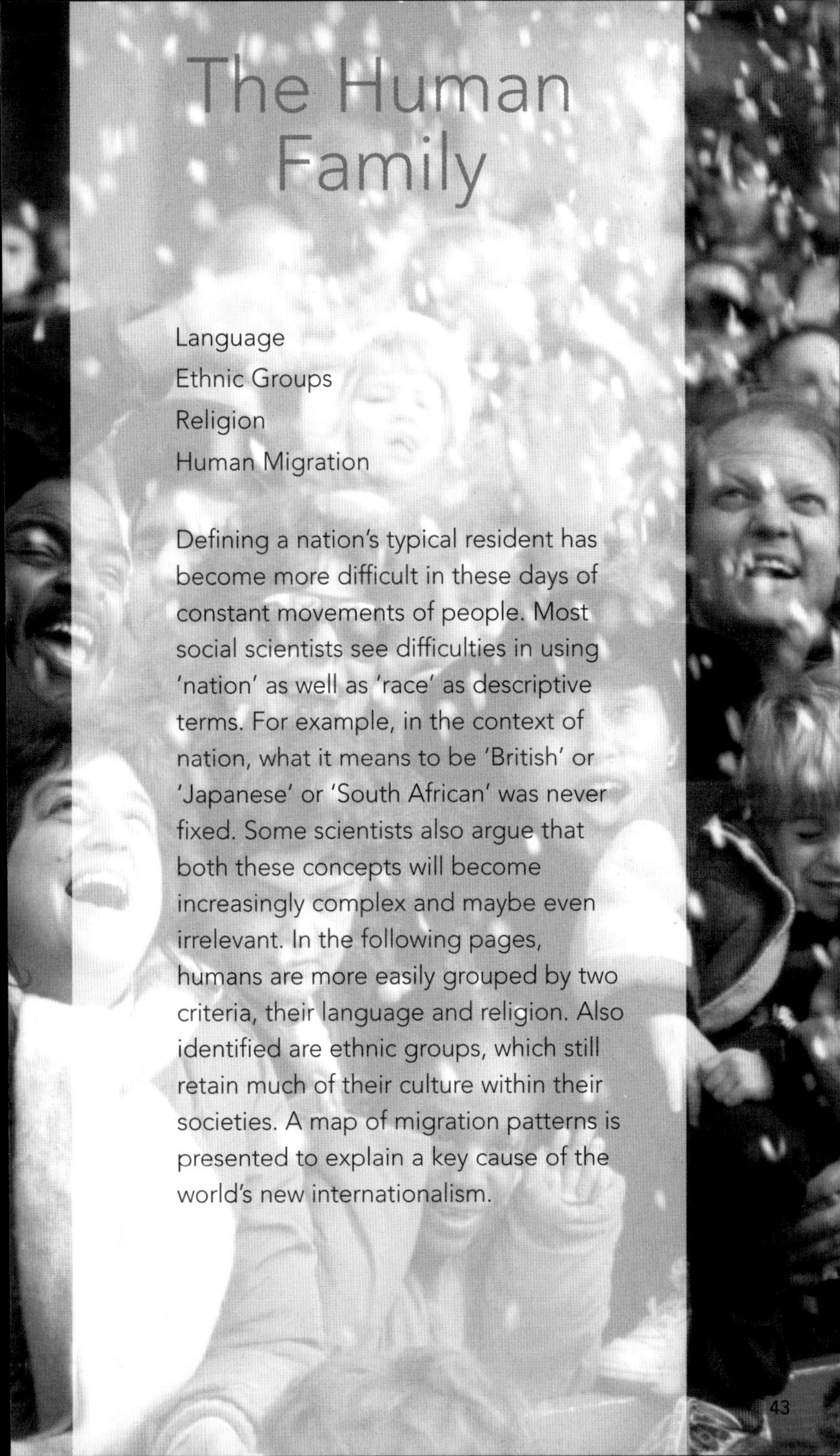

The Human Family

Language
Ethnic Groups
Religion
Human Migration

Defining a nation's typical resident has become more difficult in these days of constant movements of people. Most social scientists see difficulties in using 'nation' as well as 'race' as descriptive terms. For example, in the context of nation, what it means to be 'British' or 'Japanese' or 'South African' was never fixed. Some scientists also argue that both these concepts will become increasingly complex and maybe even irrelevant. In the following pages, humans are more easily grouped by two criteria, their language and religion. Also identified are ethnic groups, which still retain much of their culture within their societies. A map of migration patterns is presented to explain a key cause of the world's new internationalism.

LANGUAGE

The amazing diversity of language is displayed on the map and pie chart. The matching colors on the map, especially in the Western Hemisphere, Australia and New Zealand, quickly identify the directions taken by European powers in the colonial era. History also has determined the importance of languages on the world scene, especially in business and politics. Although Mandarin Chinese is by far the most spoken tongue and Spanish is second, English has become the true international language due to first the British Empire and then mainly to American influence. A few languages are not part of any of the language families listed on the next page. Basque, for example, is spoken in Spain and France but has no apparent links with any other language, living or dead. Most modern languages, of course, have acquired enormous quantities of vocabulary from one another.

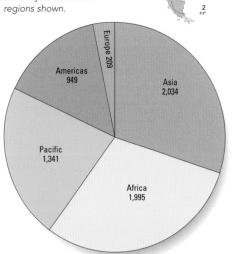

OFFICIAL LANGUAGES

First-language speakers, in millions

Mandarin Chinese	885
Spanish	332
English	322
Bengali	189
Hindi	182
Portugese	170
Russian	170
Japanese	125
German	98
Wu Chinese	77
Javanese	76
Korean	75
French	72
Vietnamese	68
Yue Chinese	66
Marathi	65
Tamil	63
Turkish	59
Urdu	58

▼ DISTRIBUTION OF LIVING LANGUAGES

The figures refer to the number of languages currently in use in the regions shown.

Europe 209

Americas 949

Asia 2,034

Pacific 1,341

Africa 1,995

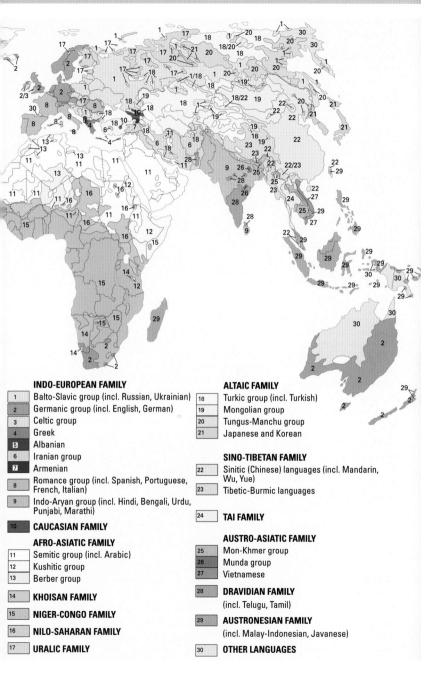

INDO-EUROPEAN FAMILY

1	Balto-Slavic group (incl. Russian, Ukrainian)
2	Germanic group (incl. English, German)
3	Celtic group
4	Greek
5	Albanian
6	Iranian group
7	Armenian
8	Romance group (incl. Spanish, Portuguese, French, Italian)
9	Indo-Aryan group (incl. Hindi, Bengali, Urdu, Punjabi, Marathi)

10 CAUCASIAN FAMILY

AFRO-ASIATIC FAMILY

11	Semitic group (incl. Arabic)
12	Kushitic group
13	Berber group

14 KHOISAN FAMILY

15 NIGER-CONGO FAMILY

16 NILO-SAHARAN FAMILY

17 URALIC FAMILY

ALTAIC FAMILY

18	Turkic group (incl. Turkish)
19	Mongolian group
20	Tungus-Manchu group
21	Japanese and Korean

SINO-TIBETAN FAMILY

| 22 | Sinitic (Chinese) languages (incl. Mandarin, Wu, Yue) |
| 23 | Tibetic-Burmic languages |

24 TAI FAMILY

AUSTRO-ASIATIC FAMILY

25	Mon-Khmer group
26	Munda group
27	Vietnamese

28 DRAVIDIAN FAMILY
(incl. Telugu, Tamil)

29 AUSTRONESIAN FAMILY
(incl. Malay-Indonesian, Javanese)

30 OTHER LANGUAGES

The use of the term 'ethnic group' as a classification is problematic in that it implies that populations can be divided into clearly identified groups. The reality is much more complex. For the purpose of this map, the term 'ethnic group' describes the different populations of a single country who share similar cultural practices. These can be indigenous groups such as the Quechua and Aymara in Bolivia, or can be migrant groups and their descendents, such as the Germans and Italians in Canada.

The Unrepresented Nations and Peoples Organisation (UNPO) is important for providing some idea of how a world political map based on recognized independent states ignores people and ethnic groups who may not feel themselves to be a part of the state in which they live. There are many more groups like this in the world who are not currently members of the UNPO.

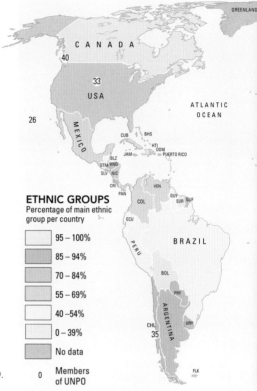

ETHNIC GROUPS
Percentage of main ethnic group per country

	95 – 100%
	85 – 94%
	70 – 84%
	55 – 69%
	40 –54%
	0 – 39%
	No data
0	Members of UNPO

Members of the Unrepresented Nations and Peoples Organisation (UNPO)

1 **Abkhazia** Autonomous republic of Georgia. Pop. est 516,000.

2 **Aboriginals of Australia** Pop. *c.*300,000.

3 **Acheh** Located in N Sumatra. Pop. *c.*25,000,000.

4 **Ahwazi** Province in SW Iran. Pop. *c.*5,000,000.

5 **Albanians in Macedonia** Pop. *c.*440,000 (21% total).

6 **Assyria** Ancient Assyria covers N Iraq, N Iran, SE Turkey and S Syria. Pop. *c.*3,300,000.

7 **Bashkortostan** Republic in the Russian federation. Pop. *c.*4,000,000.

8 **Batwa** Before the genocide, *c.*29,000 indigenous Batwa (Twa) in Rwanda. Now *c.*10–20,000.

9 **Bougainville** Island territory of Papua New Guinea. Pop *c.*204,800.

10 **Buryatia** Republic in the Russian Federation. Pop. *c.*450,000.

11 **Cabinda** Province of Angola. Pop. est. 208,900.

12 **Chechen Republic of Ichkeria** The Russian government does not recognize Chechen claims of independence. Pop. est. 573,900.

13 **Chin** Tribes of Mongol descent in Burma (Myanmar). Pop. *c.*500,000.

14 **Chittagong Hill Tracts** Situated in the SE corner of Bangladesh, the area is home to *c.*13 indigenous groups. The CHT seek autonomy from Bangladesh. Pop est. 974,445 (51% indigenous).

15 **Chuvash** Autonomous republic in the Russian Federation. Pop. *c.*1,400,000 (68% Chuvash).

16 **Circassia** There are 3,000,000 Circassians in 50 countries. 10% population of Circassia are ethnic Circassians.

17 **Cordillera** Gran Cordillera mountain range on Luzon island is the ancestral domain of the Igorots 'people from the mountains'. Pop. *c.*1,100,000 (*c.*2% of Philippine population).

18 **Crimean Tatars** Crimean pop. 2,031,000 (6% Tatars).

19 **East Turkistan** Historic region. Pop. *c.*16,000,000, (indigenous 7,200,000, Chinese 6,400,000).

20 **Gagauzia** Autonomous region of Moldova. Pop. est.169,300.

21 **Greek minority in Albania** (Northern Epiros.) Pop. *c.*280,000.

22 **Hungarian minority in Romania** The majority live in the region of Transylvania. Pop. *c.*1,519,000 (7% total pop.).

23 **Ingushetia** Autonomous Russian republic. Pop. est. 488,200.

24 **Inkeri** Ingerian Finns on Scandinavian peninsula. Pop. *c.*90,000.

25 **Iraqi Turkoman** The Turkmen are the third largest ethnic group in Iraq. Pop. est. 2,500,000.

26 **Ka Lahui Hawaii** Ka Lahui Hawaii is committed to reestablishing self-government. Pop. 1,211,537 (20% claim Hawaiian ancestory).

27 **Karenni State** The Karen are the oldest indigenous inhabitants of present day Burma (with the Mon). Pop. *c.*300,000 (7% of total).

28 **Khmer Krom** Kampuchea-Krom was the southernmost territory of the Khmer Empire. Pop. *c.*8,000,000 Khmers.

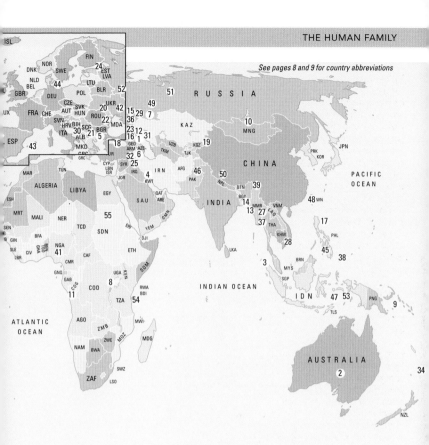

See pages 8 and 9 for country abbreviations

Komi Republic in the Russian Federation. Pop. c.1,250,000 (over 70 ethnic groups, 23% indigenous Komi).

Kosovo Autonomous province in Serbia. Pop. c.2,222,000 (80% Albanian).

Kumyk Indigenous people, mainly in the Russian republic of Dagestan (83%). Pop. c.300,000.

Kurdistan Homeland of the Kurds, a largely rural Islamic population, spread over Iran, Iraq, Turkey, and Syria. Pop. c.18,000,000.

Lakota The Lakota, Nakota and Dakota Nation (also known as the Great Sioux Nation) descends from Native Americans. Pop. c.100,000.

Maohi Indigenous people of French Polynesia. Pop. c.420,000 (70% of total).

Mapuche Indigenous people of Chile. Pop. c.1,500,000.

Mari An autonomous republic in the Russian Federation. Pop. c.750,000.

Mon The former Monland covers lower Burma (Myanmar). 4,000,000 people consider themselves Mon. Mon State pop. c.1,000,000.

Montagnards Mountain-dwelling tribes in the Vietnamese central highlands.

Nagalim Covers parts of China, India and Burma. Today there are 16 major and 20 minor tribes. Pop. c.3,000,000.

Nuxalk Indigenous peoples. About 900 Nuxalkmc live on reserves in Bella Coola Valley, approx. 560 km NW of Vancouver, Canada.

Ogoni The Ogoni have lived in the Niger Delta for over 500 years. Pop. c.500,000

Rusyn In Europe, the Carpatho-Rusyns live in Subcarpathian Rus' (Ruthenia), now Transcarpathian Region, Ukraine. Pop. est. 1,600,000 worldwide. (45% Ukraine, 38% USA, 8% Slovakia, 4% Poland).

Sanjak Situated on the Balkan peninsula. Pop. c.530,000

Scania Situated on the Scandinavian peninsula. Pop. c.1,500,000.

Shan Situated in NE Burma. Pop. c.7–8,000,000, (majority are Tai).

Sindh Second largest province in Pakistan. Sindhi pop. c.15.669,000 (12% total pop.).

South Moluccas Homeland consists of some 150 islands located in the Banda Sea. Pop. c.1,000,000.

Taiwan Officially Republic of China. Pop. 22,167,159

Tatarstan Autonomous region in the Russian Federation, populated mainly by Tatars. Pop. 3,778,600.

Tibet Autonomous region in SW China. Pop. 2,620,000.

Tuva The republic of Tuva is situated in Siberia, Russia. Pop. c.310,000 (97% Tuvans).

Udmurt Republic in the Russian Federation. Pop. c.1,644,000.

West Papua Province of Indonesia (Irian Jaya). Pop. 1,691,800, (50% indigenous).

Zanzibar Island region of Tanzania. Pop. est. 934,400.

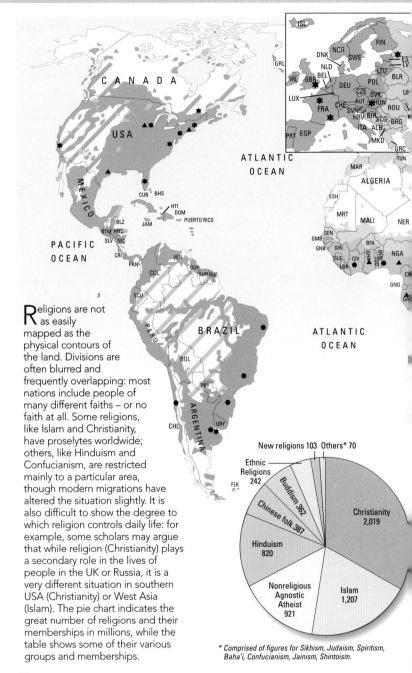

Religions are not as easily mapped as the physical contours of the land. Divisions are often blurred and frequently overlapping: most nations include people of many different faiths – or no faith at all. Some religions, like Islam and Christianity, have proselytes worldwide; others, like Hinduism and Confucianism, are restricted mainly to a particular area, though modern migrations have altered the situation slightly. It is also difficult to show the degree to which religion controls daily life: for example, some scholars may argue that while religion (Christianity) plays a secondary role in the lives of people in the UK or Russia, it is a very different situation in southern USA (Christianity) or West Asia (Islam). The pie chart indicates the great number of religions and their memberships in millions, while the table shows some of their various groups and memberships.

New religions 103   Others* 70
Ethnic Religions 242
Buddism 362
Chinese folk 387
Hinduism 820
Nonreligious Agnostic Atheist 921
Christianity 2,019
Islam 1,207

* Comprised of figures for Sikhism, Judaism, Spiritism, Baha'i, Confucianism, Jainism, Shintoism.

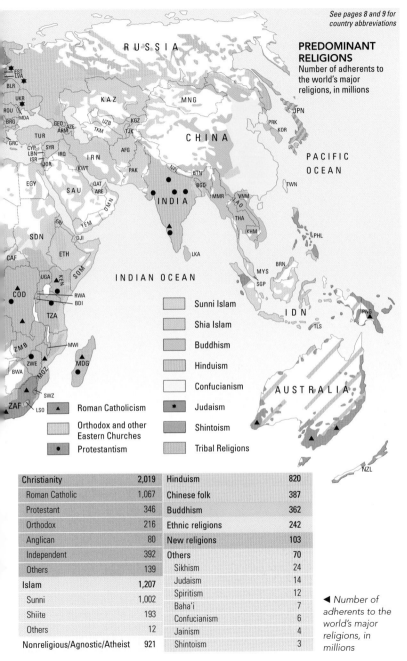

See pages 8 and 9 for country abbreviations

PREDOMINANT RELIGIONS
Number of adherents to the world's major religions, in millions

Sunni Islam
Shia Islam
Buddhism
Hinduism
Confucianism
Judaism
Shintoism
Tribal Religions

Roman Catholicism
Orthodox and other Eastern Churches
Protestantism

Christianity	2,019
Roman Catholic	1,067
Protestant	346
Orthodox	216
Anglican	80
Independent	392
Others	139
Islam	1,207
Sunni	1,002
Shiite	193
Others	12
Nonreligious/Agnostic/Atheist	921

Hinduism	820
Chinese folk	387
Buddhism	362
Ethnic religions	242
New religions	103
Others	70
Sikhism	24
Judaism	14
Spiritism	12
Baha'i	7
Confucianism	6
Jainism	4
Shintoism	3

◄ Number of adherents to the world's major religions, in millions

49

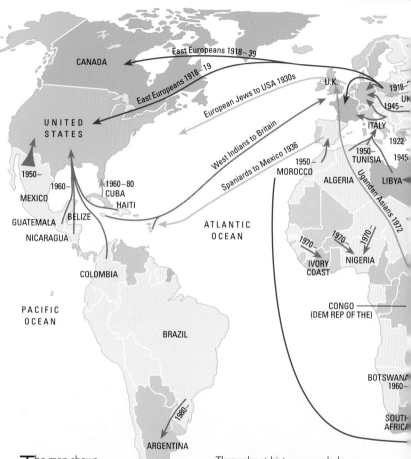

The map shows major migrations of groups of people in the 20th century. Humans have been migrating since the dawn of time, including Asians crossing the Bering Straits to America in c.9000 BC, Germanic tribes moving over the face of Europe in the 5th century, and the Maori leaving central Polynesia for New Zealand in the 14th century. These numbers are small in absolute numbers compared to modern times: more than 12 million immigrants arrived in New York between 1892 and 1924.

Throughout history, people have migrated in search of a better life and fleeing hostile conditions in their original place of inhabitation. Driving forces in the 20th century included persecution and war, such as Jews escaping the horrors of Nazism and then coming together from around the world to establish Israel. The formation and consolidation of Israel as a state in turn dispossessed Palestinians who either fled to nearby countries or lived in occupied territories. Vietnamese were also war refugees, fleeing first to France and then the USA. Colonial rule and its demise led to Indians settling in Britain,

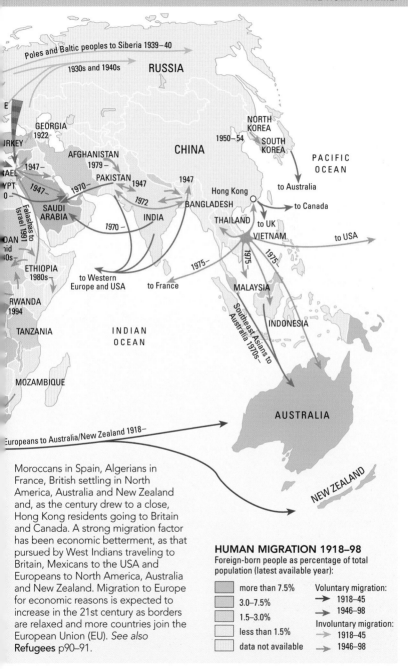

Poles and Baltic peoples to Siberia 1939–40
1930s and 1940s
RUSSIA
GEORGIA 1922
E
URKEY
AFGHANISTAN 1979–
NORTH KOREA
1950–54
SOUTH KOREA
CHINA
PACIFIC OCEAN
AEL 1947–
1970–
PAKISTAN 1947
1947
1947–
1972
Hong Kong
to Australia
YPT 0–
Falashas to Israel 1991
SAUDI ARABIA
BANGLADESH
to Canada
1970–
INDIA
THAILAND
to UK
DAN nid 0s–
VIETNAM
to USA
ETHIOPIA 1980s–
1975–
1975–
1975–
to Western Europe and USA
to France
MALAYSIA
RWANDA 1994
TANZANIA
INDIAN OCEAN
Southeast Asians to Australia 1970s–
INDONESIA
MOZAMBIQUE
AUSTRALIA
Europeans to Australia/New Zealand 1918–
NEW ZEALAND

Moroccans in Spain, Algerians in France, British settling in North America, Australia and New Zealand and, as the century drew to a close, Hong Kong residents going to Britain and Canada. A strong migration factor has been economic betterment, as that pursued by West Indians traveling to Britain, Mexicans to the USA and Europeans to North America, Australia and New Zealand. Migration to Europe for economic reasons is expected to increase in the 21st century as borders are relaxed and more countries join the European Union (EU). *See also* **Refugees** p90–91.

HUMAN MIGRATION 1918–98

Foreign-born people as percentage of total population (latest available year):

more than 7.5%	
3.0–7.5%	
1.5–3.0%	
less than 1.5%	
data not available	

Voluntary migration:
→ 1918–45
→ 1946–98

Involuntary migration:
→ 1918–45
→ 1946–98

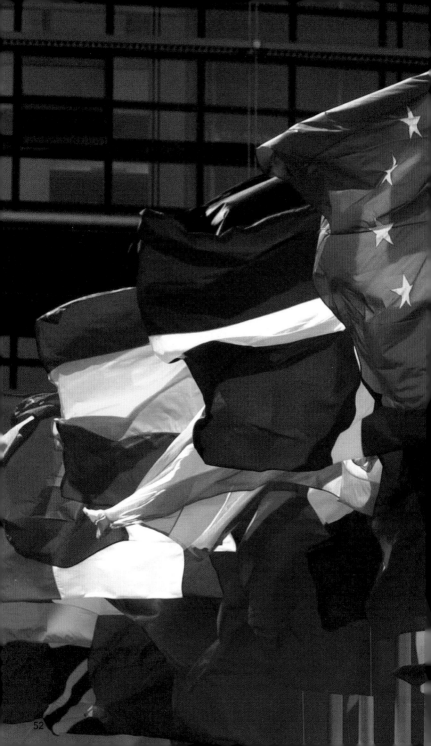

Government and Organizations

Government
Women in Parliament
United Nations Membership
United Nations Peacekeeping
Organizations

We are living in an era where electoral democracies are the norm and the elected bodies such as parliaments are becoming more inclusive as seen in the increase of their women members. These governments have an interdependent relationship with international organizations. Many organizations boost trade among the members, including the European Union (EU), the North American Free Trade Agreement (NAFTA) and the Asia-Pacific Economic Co-operation (APEC). Others, such as the United Nations, aid the developing world, and several are concerned with security, including the North Atlantic Treaty Organization (NATO) and the International Criminal Police Organization (Interpol). The importance of these relationships grows larger as the world becomes smaller.

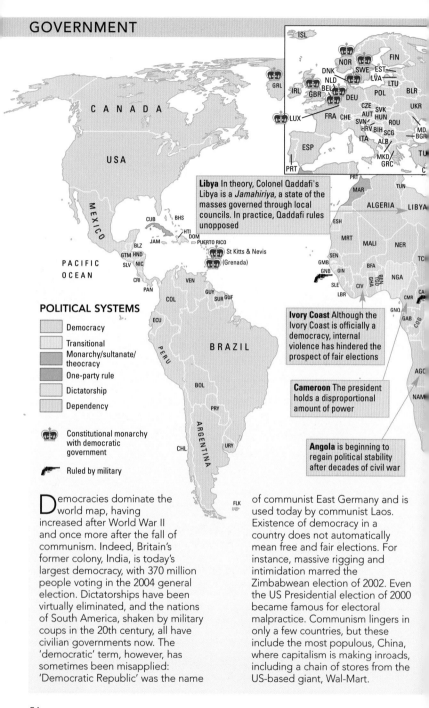

Libya In theory, Colonel Qaddafi's Libya is a *Jamahiriya*, a state of the masses governed through local councils. In practice, Qaddafi rules unopposed

POLITICAL SYSTEMS

- Democracy
- Transitional
- Monarchy/sultanate/ theocracy
- One-party rule
- Dictatorship
- Dependency

- Constitutional monarchy with democratic government
- Ruled by military

Ivory Coast Although the Ivory Coast is officially a democracy, internal violence has hindered the prospect of fair elections

Cameroon The president holds a disproportional amount of power

Angola is beginning to regain political stability after decades of civil war

Democracies dominate the world map, having increased after World War II and once more after the fall of communism. Indeed, Britain's former colony, India, is today's largest democracy, with 370 million people voting in the 2004 general election. Dictatorships have been virtually eliminated, and the nations of South America, shaken by military coups in the 20th century, all have civilian governments now. The 'democratic' term, however, has sometimes been misapplied: 'Democratic Republic' was the name of communist East Germany and is used today by communist Laos. Existence of democracy in a country does not automatically mean free and fair elections. For instance, massive rigging and intimidation marred the Zimbabwean election of 2002. Even the US Presidential election of 2000 became famous for electoral malpractice. Communism lingers in only a few countries, but these include the most populous, China, where capitalism is making inroads, including a chain of stores from the US-based giant, Wal-Mart.

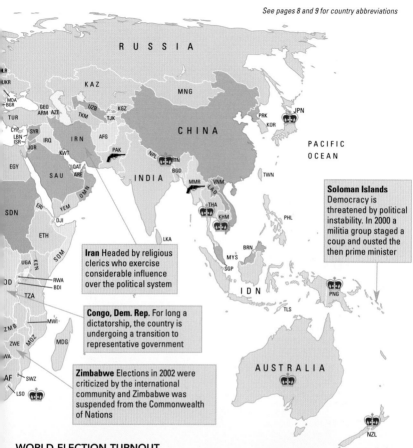

See pages 8 and 9 for country abbreviations

Iran Headed by religious clerics who exercise considerable influence over the political system

Congo, Dem. Rep. For long a dictatorship, the country is undergoing a transition to representative government

Zimbabwe Elections in 2002 were criticized by the international community and Zimbabwe was suspended from the Commonwealth of Nations

Soloman Islands Democracy is threatened by political instability. In 2000 a militia group staged a coup and ousted the then prime minister

WORLD ELECTION TURNOUT
Country vote to registration ratio, parliamentary elections

GREATEST TURNOUT (TOP TEN)			LOWEST TURNOUT (TOP TEN)		
Country	**number of elections**	**Vote**	**Country**	**number of elections**	**Vote**
Australia	22	94.5%	Mali	2	21.3%
Singapore	8	93.5%	Ivory Coast	2	37.0%
Uzbekistan	3	93.5%	Lebanon	3	39.5%
Liechtenstein*	17	92.8%	Burkina Faso	4	41.7%
Belgium**	18	92.5%	Egypt	5	45.1%
Nauru	5	92.4%	Pakistan	6	45.3%
Bahamas	6	91.5%	Mauritania	2	45.5%
Indonesia	7	91.5%	Haiti	3	47.1%
Burundi	1	91.4%	Colombia	18	47.6%
Austria	17	91.3%	Zimbabwe	3	48.7%

*Included women in the franchise from 1986.
**Included women in the franchise from 1948.

In 2004, parliaments worldwide had 6,244 women members, or 15.6% of the total, according to the Inter Parliamentary Union. As noted on the map, the Nordic countries had the most, with women making up 39.7%. Women totaled 18.4% in the Americas, 17.6% in Europe including the Nordic figure (15.9% without), 16.2% in Asia, 12.2% in the Pacific and 6.4% in Arab states. The share of women in most countries' elected bodies in Eastern Europe fell drastically after the fall of communism. Britain's first woman MP was Lady Astor in 1919 who served until 1945. By 1929, she had been joined by 13 other women in the House of Commons, which now has 118 (of 657 members). Some women have advanced to lead their nation, beginning with Sirimavo Bandaranaike in 1960 in Ceylon (now Sri Lanka), and including Britain, Canada, New Zealand, Finland, Bangladesh, India, Pakistan, Israel, Rwanda, Mozambique, Peru and Dominica. As a whole, however, women remain vastly under-represented in the world's parliaments and in decision-making roles. The GEM index on the next page lists those countries where women hold the most and least power.

See pages 8 and 9 for country abbreviations

WOMEN IN PARLIAMENT
Percentage of M.P.s who are women

- 31 – 50
- 21 – 30
- 16 – 20
- 11 – 15
- 6 – 10
- 0 – 5
- No data

BOTTOM 10 GEM INDEX		TOP 10 GEM INDEX	
1	Yemen	1	Iceland
2	Bangladesh	2	Norway
3	Egypt	3	Sweden
4	Sri Lanka	4	Denmark
5	Turkey	5	Finland
6	United Arab Emirates	6	Netherlands
7	Cambodia	7	Austria
8	South Korea	8	Germany
9	Georgia	9	Canada
10	Ukraine	10	USA

◀ The two lists rank countries by their Gender Empowerment Measure (GEM). The index attempts to measure gender inequality in three traditional areas of empowerment – economic participation and decision-making, political participation and decision-making and power over economic resources (spending power). Those countries with few to no female M.P.s tend to have particularly low ranks in the GEM index.

The United Nations was established in 1945 with 51 countries signing the charter in San Francisco, USA. This expanded to 117 by 1955, then 174 by 1992 and totaled 191 members in 2004. One of the last countries to join was Switzerland in 2002. The map shows the decades in which nations became members, and this normally followed newly acquired independence, as evidenced by African countries in the 1960s, and the former USSR republics in the 1990s. The five permanent members of the Security Council are China, France, Britain, the USA and Russia.

Although people are most aware of the UN peacekeeping missions (shown on the following pages), more than 80 percent of its budget is spent on the programs of its Economic and Social Council. Altogether, the UN consists of six main organs, 15 agencies and numerous other bodies and programs.

See pages 8 and 9 for country abbreviations

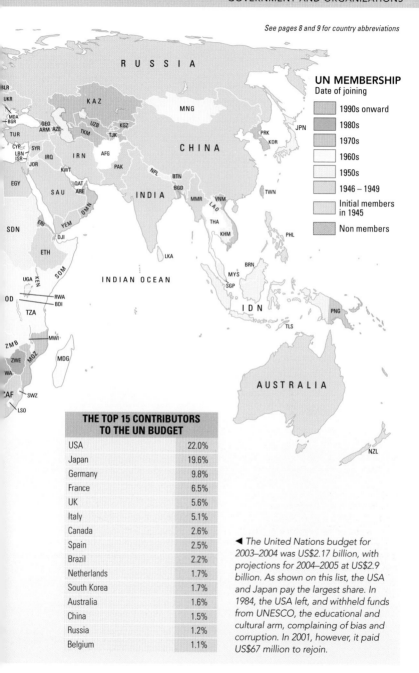

UN MEMBERSHIP
Date of joining

	1990s onward
	1980s
	1970s
	1960s
	1950s
	1946 – 1949
	Initial members in 1945
	Non members

THE TOP 15 CONTRIBUTORS TO THE UN BUDGET

USA	22.0%
Japan	19.6%
Germany	9.8%
France	6.5%
UK	5.6%
Italy	5.1%
Canada	2.6%
Spain	2.5%
Brazil	2.2%
Netherlands	1.7%
South Korea	1.7%
Australia	1.6%
China	1.5%
Russia	1.2%
Belgium	1.1%

◄ The United Nations budget for 2003–2004 was US$2.17 billion, with projections for 2004–2005 at US$2.9 billion. As shown on this list, the USA and Japan pay the largest share. In 1984, the USA left, and withheld funds from UNESCO, the educational and cultural arm, complaining of bias and corruption. In 2001, however, it paid US$67 million to rejoin.

SERBIA &
MONTENEGRO
42

CROATIA
25, 34, 37,

BOSNIA &
HERZEGOVINA
25, 36

MACEDONIA
35

CYPRUS

ATLANTIC
OCEAN

WESTERN
SAHARA
19

DOMINICAN
REPUBLIC

HONDURAS   HAITI
18   29
GUATEMALA
18, 39   NICARAGUA
EL SALVADOR 18
18, 21
COSTA RICA
18

CHA
32

SIERRA LEONE   IVORY
41, 44   COAST   CENTRA
48   AFRICA
LIBERIA   REPUBL
28   40

CONGO
5

PACIFIC
OCEAN

ATLANTIC
OCEAN

ANGO
16, 1

NAMIE
17

1   UN Truce Supervision Organization (UNTSO)
(Egypt, Israel, Jordan, Lebanon, Syria
June 1948–)

**2   UN Military Observer Group in India and
Pakistan** (UNMOGIP) (Jan 1949–)

3   First UN Emergency Force (UNEF I)
(Egypt and Israel Nov 1956–June 1967)

4   UN Observation Group in Lebanon (UNOGIL)
(June–Dec 1958)

5   UN Operation in the Congo (ONUC)
(July 1960–June 1964)

6   UN Security Force in West New Guinea
(West Irian) (UNSF) (Now Indonesia Oct 1962–Apr 1963)

7   UN Yemen Observation Mission (UNYOM)
(July 1963–Sept 1964)

8   UN Peacekeeping Force in Cyprus (UNFICYP) (Mar 1964–)

9   Mission of the Representative of the Secretary-General
in the Dominican Republic (DOMREP) (May 1965–Oct 1966)

10 UN India–Pakistan Observation Mission (UNIPOM)
(Sept 1965–Mar 1966)

11 Second UN Emergency Force (UNEF II) (Egypt and Israel
Oct 1973–July 1979)

12 UN Disengagement Observer Force (UNDOF)
(Syria June 1974–)

13 UN Interim Force in Lebanon (UNIFIL) (Mar 1978–)

14 UN Good Offices Mission in Afghanistan & Pakistan
(UNGOMAP) (Apr 1988–Mar 1990)

15 UN Iran–Iraq Military Observer Group (UNIIMOG)
(Aug 1988–Feb 1991)

16 UN Angola Verification Missions (UNAVEM I,
Jan 1988–May 1991), (II, May 1991–Feb 1995),
(III, Feb 1995–June 1997), (MONUA July 1997–Feb 1999)

17 UN Transition Assistance Group (UNTAG)
(Namibia and Angola Apr 1989–Mar 1990)

18 UN Observer Group in Central America (ONUCA)
(Costa Rica, El Salvador, Guatemala, Honduras and
Nicaragua Nov 1989–Jan 1992*)

19 UN Mission for the Referendum in Western Sahara
(MINURSO) (Sept 1991–)

20 UN Advance Mission in Cambodia (UNAMIC)
(Oct 1991–Mar 1992)

21 UN Observer Mission in El Salvador (ONUSAL)
(July 1991–Apr 1995)

22 UN Iraq–Kuwait Observation Missions (UNIKOM) (Apr 1991–)

23 UN Transitional Authority in Cambodia (UNTAC)
(Mar 1992–Sept 1993)

24 UN Operations in Somalia (UNOSOM I, Apr 1992–Mar 1993),
(UNOSOM II, Mar 1993–Mar 1995)

25 UN Protection Force (UNPROFOR) (Bosnia and Herzegovina,
Croatia, The Federal Republic of Yugoslavia (Serbia and
Montenegro) and the former Yugoslav Republic of Macedonia
Mar 1992– Dec 1995)

26 UN Operation in Mozambique (ONUMOZ) (Dec 1992–Dec 1994)

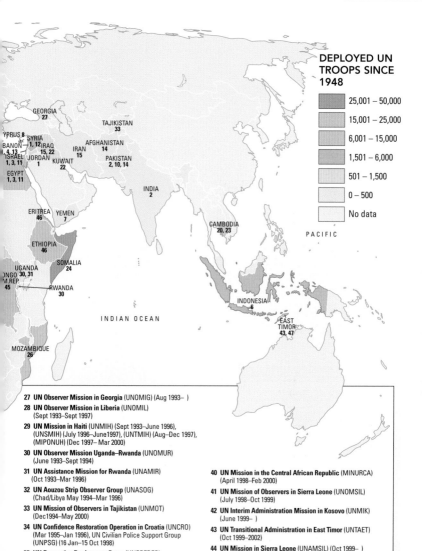

DEPLOYED UN
TROOPS SINCE
1948

- 25,001 – 50,000
- 15,001 – 25,000
- 6,001 – 15,000
- 1,501 – 6,000
- 501 – 1,500
- 0 – 500
- No data

GEORGIA 27

TAJIKISTAN 33

YPRUS 8
BANON — 1, 12 SYRIA
4, 13 IRAQ
ISRAEL JORDAN 15, 22
1, 3, 11 1 KUWAIT
22

AFGHANISTAN
14

IRAN
15

PAKISTAN
2, 10, 14

EGYPT
1, 3, 11

INDIA
2

ERITREA YEMEN
46 7

CAMBODIA
20, 23

ETHIOPIA
46

PACIFIC

UGANDA 30, 31
ONGO M.REP.
45

SOMALIA
24

RWANDA
30

INDONESIA
6

INDIAN OCEAN

EAST
TIMOR
43, 47

MOZAMBIQUE
26

27 **UN Observer Mission in Georgia** (UNOMIG) (Aug 1993–)

28 **UN Observer Mission in Liberia** (UNOMIL)
(Sept 1993–Sept 1997)

29 **UN Mission in Haiti** (UNMIH) (Sept 1993–June 1996),
(UNSMIH) (July 1996–June1997), (UNTMIH) (Aug–Dec 1997),
(MIPONUH) (Dec 1997– Mar 2000)

30 **UN Observer Mission Uganda–Rwanda** (UNOMUR)
(June 1993–Sept 1994)

31 **UN Assistance Mission for Rwanda** (UNAMIR)
(Oct 1993–Mar 1996)

32 **UN Aouzou Strip Observer Group** (UNASOG)
(Chad/Libya May 1994–Mar 1996)

33 **UN Mission of Observers in Tajikistan** (UNMOT)
(Dec1994–May 2000)

34 **UN Confidence Restoration Operation in Croatia** (UNCRO)
(Mar 1995–Jan 1996), UN Civilian Police Support Group
(UNPSG) (16 Jan–15 Oct 1998)

35 **UN Preventive Deployment Force** (UNPREDEP)
(Former Yugoslav Republic of Macedonia Mar 1995–1999)

36 **UN Mission in Bosnia–Herzegovina** (UNMIBH)
(Dec 1995–Dec 2002)

37 **Transitional Administration for Eastern Slavonia, Baranja, and
Western Sirmium** (UNTAES) (Croatia Jan 1996– Jan 1998)

38 **UN Mission of Observers in Prevlaka** (UNMOP)
(Feb 1996–Dec 2002)

39 **UN Human Rights Verification Mission in Guatemala**
(MINUGUA) (Jan–May 1997)

40 **UN Mission in the Central African Republic** (MINURCA)
(April 1998–Feb 2000)

41 **UN Mission of Observers in Sierra Leone** (UNOMSIL)
(July 1998–Oct 1999)

42 **UN Interim Administration Mission in Kosovo** (UNMIK)
(June 1999–)

43 **UN Transitional Administration in East Timor** (UNTAET)
(Oct 1999–2002)

44 **UN Mission in Sierra Leone** (UNAMSIL) (Oct 1999–)

45 **UN Organization Mission in the Democratic Republic of
Congo** (MONUC) (Nov 1999–)

46 **UN Mission In Ethiopia and Eritrea** (UNMEE) (July 2000–)

47 **UN Mission of Support in East Timor** (UNMISET) (May
2002–)

48 **UN Mission in Cote d'Ivoire** (MINUCI) (May 2003–)

** The country data shown on the map includes a total figure
for Central America*

The League of Nations was established after World War I to help maintain world peace. Despite the failure of the League to prevent World War II, it popularized the idea that a world organization could help bring order to international affairs. Since World War II, there has been an explosion of such organizations, beginning with the United Nations in 1945 for peace and negotiations. The eight organizations on this map mostly promote trade and cooperation between members in the political, economic and social areas. As they acquire more members, the world seems smaller and more manageable. Ten new nations joined the European Union's original 15 in 2004 to create the world's largest trading bloc with a population of some 455 million, and more countries are seeking membership. Another alliance of common interests is the Commonwealth of Independent States made up of 12 of the 15 former Soviet republics. As the size and power of organizations such as the EU grows, other organizations such as EFTA diminish in size.

See pages 8 and 9 for country abbreviations

ORGANIZATIONS

- OAS
- CIS
- Arab League
- AU
- EU
- EFTA
- ASEAN
- No membership

INTERNATIONAL ORGANIZATIONS

OAS Organization of American States (formed 1948). It aims to promote social and economic cooperation between countries in the developed North America and developing Latin America.

CIS The Commonwealth of Independent States (formed in 1991) comprises the countries of the former Soviet Union except for Estonia, Latvia and Lithuania.

Arab League (formed in 1945) Aims to promote economic, social, political and military cooperation.

AU In 2002, the African Union replaced the Organization of African Unity (formed 1963). The new organization aims to attract foreign investment in the 53 member states and promote social, economic and military cooperation.

EU The European Union evolved from the European Community (EC) in 1993. The original body, the European Coal and Steel Community (ECSC), was created in 1951 following the signing of the Treaty of Paris. The members of the EU aim to integrate economies, coordinate social developments and bring about political union. These members share agricultural and industrial policies and tariffs on trade. (Applicant countries in 2004: Bulgaria, Romania, Turkey)

EFTA European Free Trade Association (formed in 1960). There are now only four members.

ASEAN Association of Southeast Asian Nations (formed 1967).

Worldwide organizations must constantly adjust to changing situations. NATO, for example, was established to provide a military defense against the former Soviet Union. After the breakup of the USSR, the organization turned to peacekeeping in Bosnia-Herzegovina in 1995 and then conducted military operations to prevent genocide in Kosovo in 1999. That year, it added three former Warsaw Pact members, Hungary, Poland and the Czech Republic, and in 2004 another seven former communist nations joined: Bulgaria, Estonia, Latvia, Lithuania, Romania, Slovakia and Slovenia. Although this has worried Russia, the expansion reflects NATO's new mission of helping end localized conflicts. The oldest organization mapped here is the Commonwealth of Nations founded in 1931 to maintain cooperation among the former members of the British Empire. Although essentially a forum, in 2002 it suspended Zimbabwe for using intimidation and violence against its people. In 2003, Zimbabwe withdrew its membership.

See pages 8 and 9 for country abbreviations

ORGANIZATIONS

- OPEC
- NATO
- ACP
- LAIA
- OECD
- Commonwealth
- None of the above

INTERNATIONAL ORGANIZATIONS

OPEC Organization of Petroleum Exporting Countries (formed in 1960). It controls OPEC's eleven Members who collectively supply about 40 percent of the world's oil output, and possess more than three-quarters of the world's total proven crude oil reserves.

NATO North Atlantic Treaty Organization (formed in 1949). NATO is comprised of 26 countries across North America and Europe committed to the defense of member states.

ACP African-Caribbean-Pacific (formed in 1963). Members enjoy close economic ties with Europe.

LAIA The Latin American Integration Association (formed 1960, Spanish ALADI) superceded the Latin American Free Trade Association formed in 1961. Its aim is to promote freer regional trade.

OECD Organization for Economic Co-operation and Development (formed in 1961). It comprises 30 free-market economies. The 'G8' is its 'inner group' of leading industrial nations, comprising Canada, France, Germany, Italy, Japan, Russia, UK and the USA.

Commonwealth The Commonwealth of Nations evolved from the British Empire; it comprises 53 developed and developing nations around the world.

Crime and Punishment

Prisons
The Death Penalty
Murder
Crime
Drugs

Rising prison populations indicate both an increase in crime and the determination of courts to stem this through custodial sentences. The imposition of a 'zero tolerance' arrest policy for antisocial behavior in New York has changed that once-dangerous city into a relatively safe one. Much harsher punishment, such as the death penalty, has often proven a poor deterrent for murders. Many general crimes result from the use of alcohol or drugs, with many abusers of the latter forced into criminal activities to pay for their habits. However, these individual crime figures pale in comparison to crimes committed by states (for instance, war crimes and crimes against humanity committed by the Nazis). There is also an increasing recognition of white collar crimes and corporate crimes.

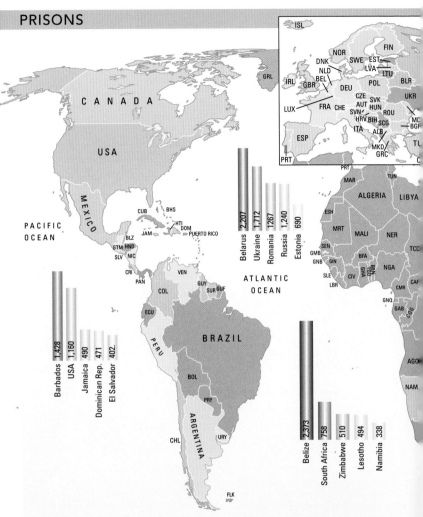

Prison populations continue to expand, resulting in crowded conditions worldwide. Figures released in 2004 by the International Centre for Prison Studies at the University of London show prison occupancy at 112.7% in England and Wales, 106.4% in the USA, 105.9% in Australia and 99.1% in New Zealand. Other research reveals the US population increased 82% between 1990 and 2002 and stood at over 2 million in 2004. If this continues, the US Department of Justice predicts the federal prisoner population will have increased by 50% between 2000 and 2007. On the map, the bar charts for each continent show the five nations with the most prisoners per prison, per 100,000 people. Such overcrowding has major implications for prisoner mental and personal health and spreads disease, including tuberculosis (occurring 100 times more in prisons than in the general population) and HIV/AIDS.

See pages 8 and 9 for country abbreviations

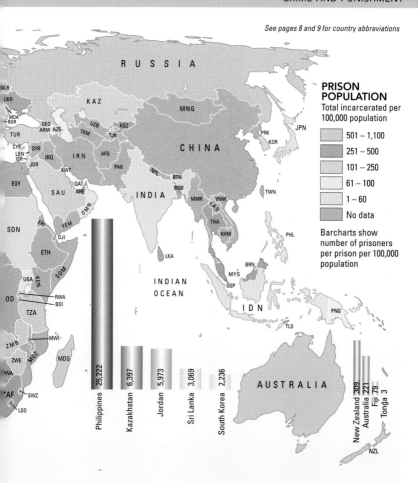

PRISON POPULATION

Total incarcerated per 100,000 population

- 501 – 1,100
- 251 – 500
- 101 – 250
- 61 – 100
- 1 – 60
- No data

Barcharts show number of prisoners per prison per 100,000 population

Philippines 25,222
Kazakhstan 6,397
Jordan 5,973
Sri Lanka 3,069
South Korea 2,236

New Zealand 309
Australia 221
Fiji 79
Tonga 3

MOST CONVICTED FEMALES	
prisoners per 100,000 population	
Belize	65.4
USA	29.7
Belarus	26.4
Ukraine	22.4
Hong Kong (China)	22.4
Kazakhstan	18.4
Malaysia	15.1
Lesotho	14.1
Kyrgyzstan	14.1
Singapore	13.3

MOST CONVICTED JUVENILES	
admitted to prison per 100,000 population	
Belize	118.4
Swaziland	66.4
Namibia	44.7
USA	38.4
South Africa	28.9
Brunei	25.1
Samoa	25.0
Lesotho	24.4
United Kingdom	18.3
Botswana	18.1

THE DEATH PENALTY

Since World War II, the worldwide trend has been to abolish the death penalty, and there are now 117 nations that have stopped executions by law or practice. Capital punishment was banned in Sweden in 1921, Britain in 1965, Canada in 1976, France in 1981 and Australia in 1985. The US Supreme Court made it illegal only from 1972 to 1976. Twelve US states continue to ban executions, and in 2004 the governor of Illinois commuted all 171 death sentences after new evidence proved the innocence of 13 prisoners on death row. Despite this, most US states continue with the death penalty.

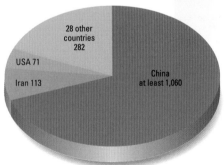

Executions per year

Only three nations stand out in this pie chart, based on statistics from Amnesty International. Many people believe China's true figure is much higher. The USA conducted 820 executions from 1977–2002, with more than a third occurring in Texas.

▶ *The table on the following page reveals that 31 nations practiced capital punishment in 2002, only one less than 10 years earlier. Amnesty International also recorded 1,146 executions in 2003, with 84% of them taking place in China, Iran, the USA and Vietnam. The USA carried out its 900th execution on March 3 2004 since the death sentence became legal again in 1976. Some 3,500 US prisoners were under sentence of death in 2004.*

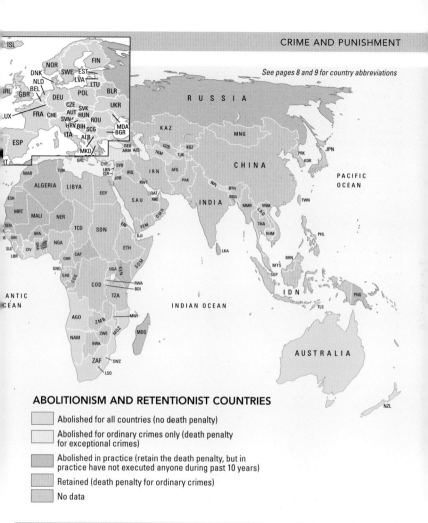

See pages 8 and 9 for country abbreviations

ABOLITIONISM AND RETENTIONIST COUNTRIES

Abolished for all countries (no death penalty)

Abolished for ordinary crimes only (death penalty for exceptional crimes)

Abolished in practice (retain the death penalty, but in practice have not executed anyone during past 10 years)

Retained (death penalty for ordinary crimes)

No data

RECORDED WORLDWIDE EXECUTIONS BY YEAR (1993–2002)				
Year	Countries carrying out executions	Executions recorded	Countries with over 100 executions	% of recorded executions in countries with over 100 executions
1993	32	1,831	1	77%
1994	37	2,331	3	87%
1995	41	3,276	3	85%
1996	39	4,272	4	92%
1997	40	2,607	3	82%
1998	37	2,258	2	72%
1999	31	1,813	4	80%
2000	28	1,457	2	77%
2001	31	3,048	2	86%
2002	31	1,526	2	77%

The world map shows the number of reported murders per 100,000 people in each country, with Honduras and South Africa having the highest rates. Specific national figures are given in the lists based on the Interpol International Crime Statistics. In 2002, England and Wales had 1,048 murders with 87% solved, while Russia had 32,285 murders and 77% solved. France recorded 2,173 murders in 2003 with 81% solved. Although the USA had 16,204 homicides in 2002, many being gun deaths, the map reveals that America's reported murder rate for its population is similar to those of European countries and Australia, although only 64% of the US murders were solved. Several countries have experienced a fall in the homicide rate. Canada, for instance had 3.1 murders per 100,000 population in 1975 and only 1.9 in 2002. It is worth noting that the murder rates given here are based on the number of reported murders, that is, those murders recorded by the police. The actual murder rate for some countries may be much higher.

See pages 8 and 9 for country abbreviations

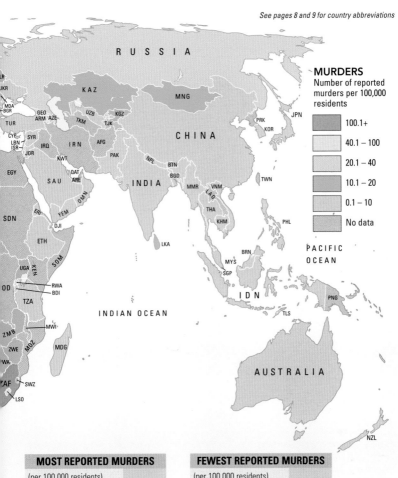

MURDERS

Number of reported murders per 100,000 residents

	100.1+
	40.1 – 100
	20.1 – 40
	10.1 – 20
	0.1 – 10
	No data

MOST REPORTED MURDERS		FEWEST REPORTED MURDERS	
(per 100,000 residents)		(per 100,000 residents)	
Honduras	154.0	Syria	1.0
South Africa	114.8	Niger	0.9
Georgia	83.7	Oman	0.9
Colombia	70.0	Indonesia	0.8
Lesotho	50.4	Mauritania	0.8
Rwanda	45.1	Gambia, The	0.7
Jamaica	43.7	Mali	0.7
El Salvador	34.3	Senegal	0.6
Venezuela	33.2	Burkina Faso	0.4
Bolivia	32.0	Cameroon	0.4

The surprising information on this map is that the UK, Sweden, Finland and New Zealand are among those nations with the highest recorded crime rates in the world. Sweden, as the rankings on the following page show, has the most recorded crimes per 100,000 people. In 2003, these included 8,618 thefts and 1,802 instances of breaking into a building to commit burglary. Crime in England and Wales, despite being high, fell by 3% in 2002–2003, according to the British Crime Survey, including a 14% drop in robberies. Australia also experienced a 29% decline in robberies from 2001 to 2003. In the USA, violent crime fell 0.9% in 2002,

with an estimated 1.4 million offenses. This is 25.9% lower than the 1993 figure. Many countries now include information on computer security incidents and other types of cybercrime. As noted on pages 72–73, reported crime statistics are not always a good indication of actual crime rates, but may be more an indication of the willingness of the population to report a crime. High reported crime rates may also demonstrate the efficiency of the police force in recording crimes.

It is worth noting that what is 'crime' is not fixed but changes with time and place. For instance, domestic abuse has only recently been recognized as a crime in the UK.

See pages 8 and 9 for country abbreviations

RECORDED CRIME
Police statistics per
100,000 population

	9,001+
	3,001 – 9,000
	1,001 – 3,000
	301 – 1,000
	10 – 300
	0/No data

▼ This list is led by Sweden with about
1.2 million crimes reported each year.

MOST RECORDED CRIMES		FEWEST RECORDED CRIMES	
per 100,000 population		per 100,000 population	
Sweden	13,516	Syria	17
Guyana	12,400	Egypt	37
New Zealand	11,153	Indonesia	80
Dominica	10,763	Madagascar	83
Finland	10,243	China	131
Bermuda	9,966	Philippines	136
United Kingdom	9,767	Yemen	138
Denmark	9,450	Iraq	149
Chile	9,276	Azerbaijan	173
USA	8,517	India	177

DRUGS

Drug abuse involved 4.7% of the world's population in 2002, according to estimates by the United Nations Office of Drugs and Crime (UNDOC). The previous year's figure was 4.3%, with the increase primarily a result of more widespread cannabis abuse. The pie chart indicates that cannabis is by far the most popular choice of all drug users. By 2002, cannabis users numbered around 160 million people, or 3.9% of the global population. The next largest drug group, 34 million people or 0.8% of the population, used amphetamine-type stimulants (ATS), followed by 14.9 million using opiates (of which 9.5 million used heroin) and 14.1 million using cocaine. Drug users often tend to use more than one drug and so the total number of drug users worldwide is probably much lower than indicated.

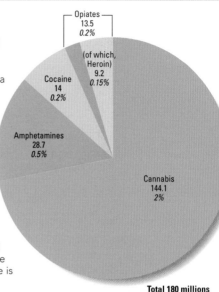

Total 180 millions
3% of global population

▲ *Estimated number of drug users per year in millions. Figures in italic denote percentage of global population*

▶ **Coca leaf production** *(in metric tonnes) The two pie charts indicate how Colombia replaced Peru in the 1990s as the major grower of coca leaf. Colombia now produces 75% of the global crop. The bar chart below compares opium poppy production during the 1990s. By 2002, an estimated 4,140 metric tonnes (4,600 tons) was produced worldwide, with 75% being grown in Afghanistan.*

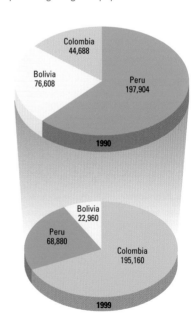

▼ **Main five cultivators of opium poppies**

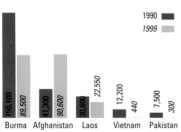

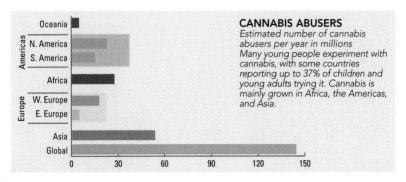

CANNABIS ABUSERS
Estimated number of cannabis abusers per year in millions
Many young people experiment with cannabis, with some countries reporting up to 37% of children and young adults trying it. Cannabis is mainly grown in Africa, the Americas, and Asia.

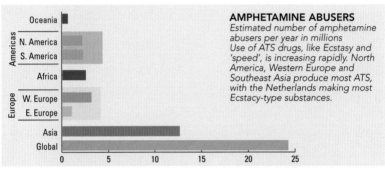

AMPHETAMINE ABUSERS
Estimated number of amphetamine abusers per year in millions
Use of ATS drugs, like Ecstasy and 'speed', is increasing rapidly. North America, Western Europe and Southeast Asia produce most ATS, with the Netherlands making most Ecstacy-type substances.

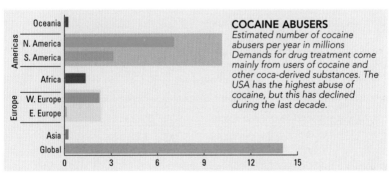

COCAINE ABUSERS
Estimated number of cocaine abusers per year in millions
Demands for drug treatment come mainly from users of cocaine and other coca-derived substances. The USA has the highest abuse of cocaine, but this has declined during the last decade.

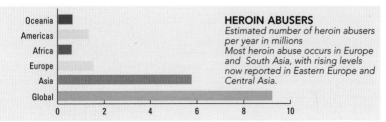

HEROIN ABUSERS
Estimated number of heroin abusers per year in millions
Most heroin abuse occurs in Europe and South Asia, with rising levels now reported in Eastern Europe and Central Asia.

Conflict

The 20th century, the age of world wars and nuclear power, introduced the fear of worldwide annihilation. This abated with the end of the Cold War, but has been replaced by terrorism and the possible use of weapons of mass destruction. Localized wars have proliferated, bringing former enemies together in the North Atlantic Treaty Organization (NATO) to attempt to bring stability to Bosnia and Herzegovina, Kosovo and Afghanistan, while the United Nations operates ongoing peacekeeping missions, totaling 15 alone in 2003. Military budgets and arms sales continue to add up to large numbers, as do the war casualties and refugees.

WAR SINCE 1945

Past Current

Major international war
Minor international war
Major civil war
Minor civil war

Arctic Circle

Tropic of Cancer

Mexico
1993–1997
Honduras/
El Salvador
1969
Cuba
1952–59
Haiti
1980, 1993
Grenada
1983
Guatemala
1960–96
Nicaragua
1972–
El Salvador
1972–92
Panama
1989
Venezuela
1962–74
Equator
Colombia
1948–69, 1976–
Peru/Ecuador
1942, 1981, 1995

Tropic of Capricorn
Chile
1973

Argentina
1977–81

Argentina/UK
(Falkland Is.)
1982

Antarctic Circle

Serbi
Bosni
Croat
1991

Algeria/France
1954–62

Western
Sahara
1973, 1980–90
Algeria 1962–65, 1992–2004
Cha
1965–
1985
Mali
1990–94
Guinea
Bissau
1963–74
Nigeria
(Biafra)
1967–70
Nigeria/
Cameroon
1980–81
Sierra
Leone
2000–
Camero
1955–5
Liberia
1989–2003
Congo
1960
Cong
(Dem.R
Zaire
1961–2
ANGOLA/
Portugal
1961
Angola
(Cabinda)
1975–
Namibia
1975–89

In the period 1946–2002 there were 226 armed conflicts according to the definitions of the Uppsala Conflict Data project. The definition of a war is problematic. When does a rebel uprising become a civil war? Some historians dispute using the term 'war on terror', and the USA has said terrorists do not have the same rights as 'real' soldiers.

The major wars since 1945 listed opposite claim the largest numbers of battle deaths. The list includes only conflicts between two organized parties. Reliable information on battle deaths is difficult to obtain, and the delineation between types of war – interstate or international – is not always clear for wars between two parts of a divided country.

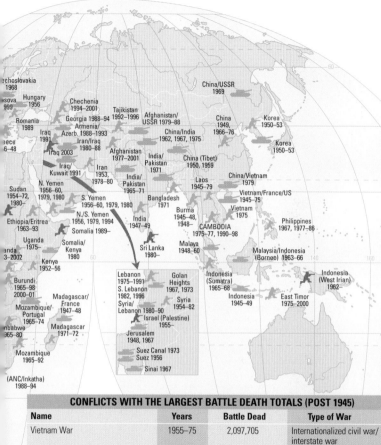

echoslovakia 1968
sova 999
Hungary 1956
Romania 1989
Chechenia 1994–2001
Tajikistan 1992–1996
China/USSR 1969
Georgia 1988–94
Afghanistan/ USSR 1979–88
Armenia/ Azerb. 1988–1993
Iraq 1991
Iran/Iraq 1980–88
Iraq 2003
China 1949, 1966–76
Korea 1950–53
Korea 1950–53
eece 6–48
Iraq/ Kuwait 1991
Iran 1953, 1978–80
China/India 1962, 1967, 1975
Afghanistan 1977–2001
India/ Pakistan 1971
China (Tibet) 1950, 1959
Sudan 1954–72, 1980–
N. Yemen 1956–60, 1979, 1980
S. Yemen 1956–60, 1979, 1980
India/ Pakistan 1965–71
Laos 1945–79
China/Vietnam 1979
Vietnam/France/US 1945–75
N./S. Yemen 1956, 1979, 1994
Bangladesh 1971
Burma 1945–48, 1948–
Vietnam 1975
Ethiopia/Eritrea 1963–93
Somalia 1989–
India 1947–49
CAMBODIA 1975–77, 1990–98
Philippines 1967, 1977–86
Uganda 1975–
anda 3–2002
Somalia/ Kenya 1980
Sri Lanka 1980–
Malaya 1948–60
Malaysia/Indonesia (Borneo) 1963–66
Kenya 1952–56
Indonesia (Sumatra) 1965–68
Indonesia (West Irian) 1962–
Burundi 1965–98 2000–01
Madagascar/ France 1947–48
Indonesia 1945–49
East Timor 1975–2000
Mozambique/ Portugal 1965–74
Madagascar 1971–72
Lebanon 1975–1991
Golan Heights 1967, 1973
nbabwe 965–80
S. Lebanon 1982, 1996
Syria/ Lebanon 1980–90
Syria 1954–82
Mozambique 1965–92
Israel (Palestine) 1955–
Jerusalem 1948, 1967
(ANC/Inkatha) 1988–94
Suez Canal 1973
Suez 1956
Sinai 1967

CONFLICTS WITH THE LARGEST BATTLE DEATH TOTALS (POST 1945)			
Name	**Years**	**Battle Dead**	**Type of War**
Vietnam War	1955–75	2,097,705	Internationalized civil war/ interstate war
Korean War	1950–53	1,251,239	Interstate war
China	1946–49	1,200,000	Civil war
Iran-Iraq War	1980–88	644,500	Interstate war
Afghanistan	1978–2002	560,000	Internationalized civil war
French Indochina War	1946–54	365,000	Colonial war
Algerian War of Independence	1954–62	252,026	Colonial war
Cambodia	1967–75	250,000	Internationalized civil war
Eritrean Independence from Ethiopia	1962–91	200,000	Civil war
Mozambique	1976–92	174,599	Civil war
Angola	1974–2002	160,475	Internationalized civil war
Greece	1946–49	154,000	Civil war
Democratic Republic of Congo	1998–2001	145,000	Internationalized civil war
Lebanon	1975–90	130,700	Internationalized civil war
Uganda	1981–89	106,000	Civil war

SIZE OF ARMIES

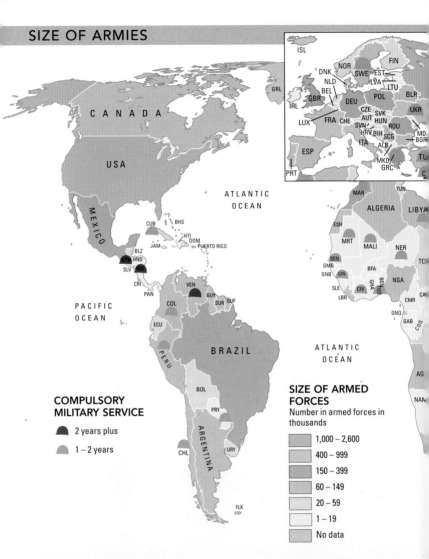

COMPULSORY MILITARY SERVICE

- 2 years plus
- 1 – 2 years

SIZE OF ARMED FORCES
Number in armed forces in thousands

- 1,000 – 2,600
- 400 – 999
- 150 – 399
- 60 – 149
- 20 – 59
- 1 – 19
- No data

The USA eliminated compulsory military service in 1973, reducing its army's strength from 1,319,735 in 1970 to 496,067 in 2003. America's fight against terrorism and other military adventures, however, has resulted in the call up of reserves and National Guard troops to increase the size of its army. The total for all of the US services in 2003 was 1.4 million troops, second to China, whose 2.3 million represent the world's largest military. National conscription was discontinued in the UK in 1962 and in Australia in 1972.

Compulsory military service continues in many countries, as the map illustrates. Not detailed on the map are those countries requiring less than one year's military service. Such countries include Austria and Finland.

See pages 8 and 9 for country abbreviations

ARMED FORCES PER CAPITA

LARGEST FORCES		SMALLEST FORCES	
North Korea	0.04	Ghana	0.0003
Israel	0.03	Niger	0.0005
United Arab Emirates	0.03	Malawi	0.0006
Greece	0.02	Mozambique	0.0007
Jordan	0.02	Kenya	0.0007
Singapore	0.02	Nigeria	0.0007
Syria	0.02	Bangladesh	0.0007
Oman	0.02	Burkina Faso	0.0007
Lebanon	0.02	Cameroon	0.0008
Iraq	0.02	Mali	0.0008

◄ North Korea conscripts four people out of every 100, the highest rate in the world. Its army, the fourth largest, had 1.1 million soldiers in 2003. South Korea, by contrast, had 686,000 military personnel.

DEFENSE SPENDING
Military expenditure as percentage of GDP

- 10–29
- 5.0–9.9
- 2.5–4.9
- 1.5–2.4
- 1.0–1.4
- 0–0.9
- No data

	TOP TEN	MILITARY BUDGET	BOTTOM TEN	
	Country	**Budget**	**Country**	**Budget**
1	USA	399.1	1	Luxembourg	0.2
2	Russia	65.0	2	Sudan	0.6
3	China	47.0	3	Serbia & Montenegro	0.7
4	Japan	42.6	4	Cuba	0.8
5	United Kingdom	38.4	5	Syria	1.0
6	France	29.5	6	Hungary	1.1
7	Germany	24.9	7	Libya	1.2
8	Saudi Arabia	21.3	8	Portugal	1.3
9	Italy	19.4	9	Philippines	1.4
10	India	15.6	10	Iraq	1.4

See pages 8 and 9 for country abbreviations

The cost of maintaining a military force is an important part of a national budget. North Korea's large standing army places a severe strain on its weak economy. The USA and Russia, as the map notes, allocate about the same percentage level of their gross domestic product (GDP), but the USA spends more than six times as much on its military. In fact, the box on the previous page shows it spends more than the next nine countries combined. Iraq, which spent US$1.4 billion before its defeat in 2003, now ranks near the bottom in expenditure for its own troops.

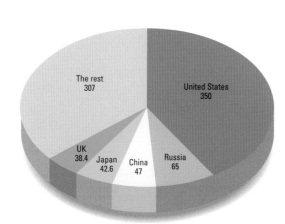

MILITARY EXPENDITURE
Proportion of the world total, US$billion

In 2003, the world was estimated to have spent US$850 billion on defense. The US was responsible for 59% of that total. The administration of President George W. Bush requested $399.1 billion for the military in fiscal year 2004.

85

ARMS

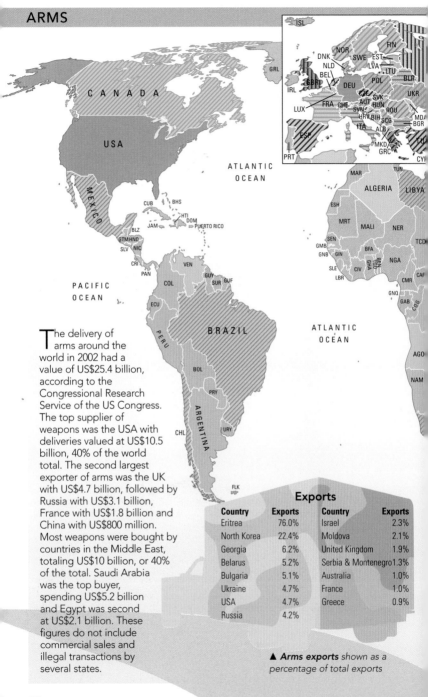

ATLANTIC OCEAN

PACIFIC OCEAN

ATLANTIC OCEAN

The delivery of arms around the world in 2002 had a value of US$25.4 billion, according to the Congressional Research Service of the US Congress. The top supplier of weapons was the USA with deliveries valued at US$10.5 billion, 40% of the world total. The second largest exporter of arms was the UK with US$4.7 billion, followed by Russia with US$3.1 billion, France with US$1.8 billion and China with US$800 million. Most weapons were bought by countries in the Middle East, totaling US$10 billion, or 40% of the total. Saudi Arabia was the top buyer, spending US$5.2 billion and Egypt was second at US$2.1 billion. These figures do not include commercial sales and illegal transactions by several states.

Exports

Country	Exports	Country	Exports
Eritrea	76.0%	Israel	2.3%
North Korea	22.4%	Moldova	2.1%
Georgia	6.2%	United Kingdom	1.9%
Belarus	5.2%	Serbia & Montenegro	1.3%
Bulgaria	5.1%	Australia	1.0%
Ukraine	4.7%	France	1.0%
USA	4.7%	Greece	0.9%
Russia	4.2%		

▲ **Arms exports** shown as a percentage of total exports

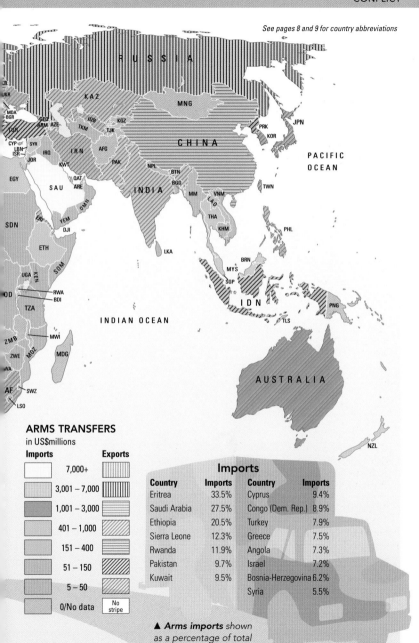

See pages 8 and 9 for country abbreviations

RUSSIA

KAZ

MNG

CHINA

JPN

PRK

KOR

PACIFIC
OCEAN

UKR

MDA
BGR

GEO
ARM AZE

UZB

KGZ

TKM

TJK

CYP
LBN
ISR

SYR

IRQ

I R N

AFG

JOR

KWT

PAK

NPL

BTN

BGD

TWN

EGY

SAU

QAT

ARE

OMN

INDIA

MM

VNM

LAO

THA

KHM

PHL

SDN

ERI

YEM

DJI

LKA

BRN

MYS

SGP

ETH

SOM

UGA

KEN

IDN

OD

RWA

BDI

TZA

INDIAN OCEAN

TLS

PNG

ZMB

MWI

ZWE

MDZ

MDG

WA

AUSTRALIA

AF

SWZ

LSO

NZL

ARMS TRANSFERS

in US$millions

Imports		Exports
	7,000+	
	3,001 – 7,000	
	1,001 – 3,000	
	401 – 1,000	
	151 – 400	
	51 – 150	
	5 – 50	
	0/No data	No stripe

Imports

Country	Imports	Country	Imports
Eritrea	33.5%	Cyprus	9.4%
Saudi Arabia	27.5%	Congo (Dem. Rep.)	8.9%
Ethiopia	20.5%	Turkey	7.9%
Sierra Leone	12.3%	Greece	7.5%
Rwanda	11.9%	Angola	7.3%
Pakistan	9.7%	Israel	7.2%
Kuwait	9.5%	Bosnia-Herzegovina	6.2%
		Syria	5.5%

▲ **Arms imports** shown as a percentage of total imports

87

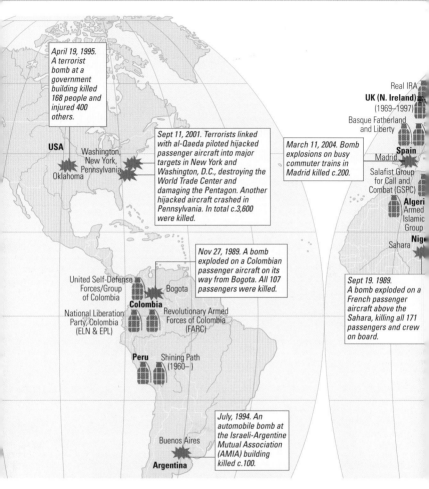

April 19, 1995. A terrorist bomb at a government building killed 168 people and injured 400 others.

USA

Washington, New York, Pennsylvania

Oklahoma

Sept 11, 2001. Terrorists linked with al-Qaeda piloted hijacked passenger aircraft into major targets in New York and Washington, D.C., destroying the World Trade Center and damaging the Pentagon. Another hijacked aircraft crashed in Pennsylvania. In total c.3,600 were killed.

Real IRA

UK (N. Ireland) (1969–1997)

Basque Fatherland and Liberty

March 11, 2004. Bomb explosions on busy commuter trains in Madrid killed c.200.

Spain

Madrid

Salafist Group for Call and Combat (GSPC)

Algeri Armed Islamic Group

Nig

Sahara

Nov 27, 1989. A bomb exploded on a Colombian passenger aircraft on its way from Bogota. All 107 passengers were killed.

Sept 19. 1989. A bomb exploded on a French passenger aircraft above the Sahara, killing all 171 passengers and crew on board.

United Self-Defense Forces/Group of Colombia

Bogota

Colombia

National Liberation Party, Colombia (ELN & EPL)

Revolutionary Armed Forces of Colombia (FARC)

Peru Shining Path (1960–)

July, 1994. An automobile bomb at the Israeli-Argentine Mutual Association (AMIA) building killed c.100.

Buenos Aires

Argentina

This map highlights the extent of terrorism around the world. Since the terrorist attacks in the USA on September 11 2001 that killed c.3,600 people in New York City, Washington D.C. and Pennsylvania, nations have greatly increased their antiterrorist organizations and international coordination. The US government passed the USA Patriot Act in 2001, enabling the government to detain noncitizen terror suspects without trial. Britain's antiterrorism legislation allows suspects to be detained for up to seven days without appearing in court. In 2003, the USA created the Department of Homeland Security, bringing together 180,000 personnel from 22 organizations. The USA, with strong British support, led military actions against governments it claimed were harboring or supporting terrorists, overthrowing the Taliban regime in Afghanistan in December 2001 and Saddam Hussein's rule in Iraq in April 2003. The US Department of State published a list in October 2003 that redesignated 25 foreign terrorist organizations, bringing the total to 36.

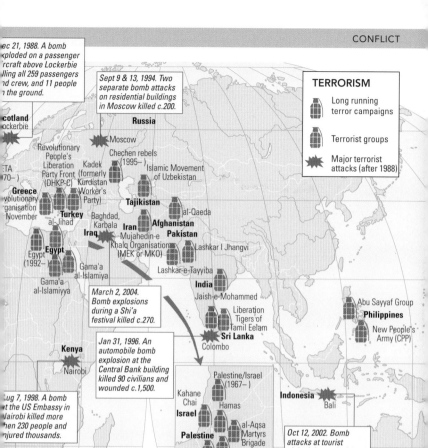

Dec 21, 1988. A bomb exploded on a passenger aircraft above Lockerbie killing all 259 passengers and crew, and 11 people on the ground.

Sept 9 & 13, 1994. Two separate bomb attacks on residential buildings in Moscow killed c.200.

TERRORISM

Long running terror campaigns

Terrorist groups

Major terrorist attacks (after 1988)

Scotland
Lockerbie

Russia

Moscow

Revolutionary People's Liberation Party Front (DHKP-C)

Kadek (formerly Kurdistan Worker's Party)

Chechen rebels (1995–)

Islamic Movement of Uzbekistan

ETA (1970–)

Greece
Revolutionary Organisation November

Tajikistan

al-Qaeda

Turkey
al-Jihad

Baghdad, Karbala

Iran

Afghanistan

Iraq

Mujahedin-e Khalq Organisation (MEK or MKO)

Pakistan

Lashkar I Jhangvi

Egypt
(1992–)

Egypt

Gama'a al-Islamia

Lashkar-e-Tayyiba

India

Gama'a al-Islamiyya

March 2, 2004. Bomb explosions during a Shi'a festival killed c.270.

Jaish-e-Mohammed

Abu Sayyaf Group

Philippines

Liberation Tigers of Tamil Eelam

New People's Army (CPP)

Kenya

Nairobi

Jan 31, 1996. An automobile bomb explosion at the Central Bank building killed 90 civilians and wounded c.1,500.

Sri Lanka
Colombo

Aug 7, 1998. A bomb at the US Embassy in Nairobi killed more then 230 people and injured thousands.

Palestine/Israel (1967–)

Kahane Chai

Israel

Hamas

Indonesia

Bali

Palestine

al-Aqsa Martyrs Brigade

Abu Nidal Organisation

Palastinian Islamic Jihad - Shaqaqi Faction

Oct 12, 2002. Bomb attacks at tourist nightclubs on the island of Bali killed c.200.

AL-QAEDA

Al-Qaeda ('The Base') is a terrorist organization established about 1998 by Osama bin Laden, a rich Saudi dissident. He has issued a 'declaration of war' against the USA. Protected by Afghanistan's Taliban regime, bin Laden constructed training camps and began bombing US targets abroad, culminating in the attacks on America on September 11 2001. After the USA overthrew the Taliban in 2001, searches for bin Laden have failed. Al-Qaeda members were scattered but continue to plot attacks, communicating with their loose network of satellite terrorist organizations in various countries. One group affliated with al-Qaeda claimed to have bombed the Madrid trains on March 11 2004, killing some 200 people.

Besides Al-Qaeda (profiled above), they include the Palestinian organization Hamas, known for its suicide attacks on Israelis, Hizballah in Lebanon; al-Jihad in Egypt and the Liberation Tigers of Tamil Eelam in Sri Lanka. However, some social scientists point out that often states themselves act in manners that blur the distinction between terrorism and counterterrorism.

REFUGEES

Refugees are the secondary victims of war. The United Nations Refugee Agency (UNHCR) recorded 10.4 million refugees at the beginning of 2003. This was down from 12 million the previous year, because nearly 2 million Afghans returned to their country (although another 2.5 million stayed in exile). The new refugee displacement for 2002 totaled nearly 300,000 people. If other displaced persons were included, such as asylum seekers or those forced to move within their own country, the figure would be 20.6 million, about one out of every 300 people on Earth.

Syria 3,000
Sri Lanka 9,000
Other 14,000
Iraq 51,000
Iran 15,000
Serbia & Montenegro 21,000
Turkey 42,000
Afghanistan 25,000

WORLD REFUGEES
Refugees per country of asylum

- 500,001 – 1,350,000
- 100,001 – 500,000
- 50,001 – 100,000
- 10,001 – 50,000
- 5,001 – 10,000
- 0 – 5,000
- No data

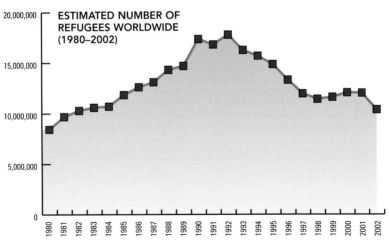

ESTIMATED NUMBER OF REFUGEES WORLDWIDE (1980–2002)

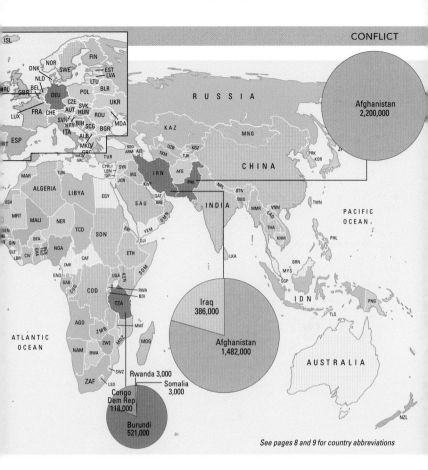

Afghanistan
2,200,000

Iraq
386,000

Afghanistan
1,482,000

Rwanda 3,000
Somalia 3,000
Congo
Dem Rep
118,000

Burundi
521,000

See pages 8 and 9 for country abbreviations

▲ *Proportion of total refugees by country of origin*

GREATEST NUMBER OF REFUGEES	
Iran	1,307,000
Pakistan	1,227,000
Germany	903,000
Tanzania	689,000
USA	485,000
Serbia and Montenegro	354,000
Congo (Dem. Rep. of the)	333,000
Sudan	328,000
China	297,000
Armenia	248,000
Zambia	247,000
Saudi Arabia	245,000
Kenya	234,000
Uganda	217,000
Guinea	182,000

◄ *The UNHCR list of countries hosting the most refugees is led by Iran and Pakistan, the destination of Afghans escaping the conflict that overthrew the Taliban regime (see Terrorism, pages 88–89). The largest new group of refugees in 2002 were some 105,000 Liberians leaving their country to avoid rebel raids. Overall, Asia has the most refugees with 4,188,100, followed by Africa with 3,343,700, Europe with 2,136,300, North America with 615,100, Oceania with 65,400, and Latin America and the Caribbean with 41,100.*

Health

Life Expectancy
Disease
HIV and AIDS
Smoking and Alcohol
Safe Water
Food Consumption

The health of a nation's population is closely linked to the strength of its economy, since this determines its ability to provide preventive health programs and proper medical treatment. Wealthy nations take clean water and healthy food for granted, but the lack of these contributes to the lower life expectancy in developing countries. An individual's life style, however, plays a key role in both wealthy and poor nations. Many diseases and deaths result from the use of tobacco and alcohol, while unsafe sex, no cure and lack of affordable medicines has led to the worldwide scourge of HIV and AIDS.

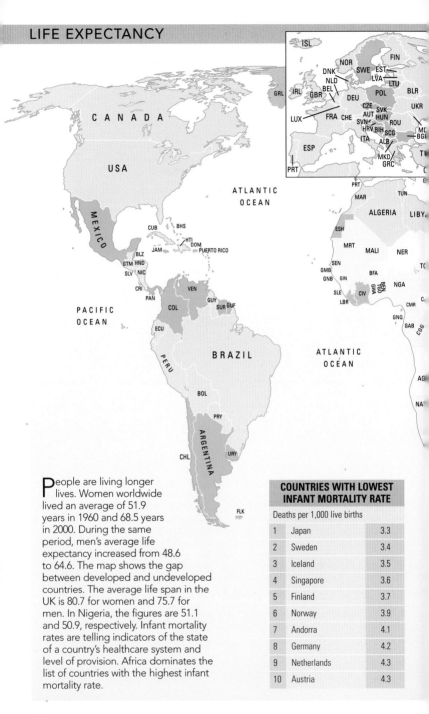

People are living longer lives. Women worldwide lived an average of 51.9 years in 1960 and 68.5 years in 2000. During the same period, men's average life expectancy increased from 48.6 to 64.6. The map shows the gap between developed and undeveloped countries. The average life span in the UK is 80.7 for women and 75.7 for men. In Nigeria, the figures are 51.1 and 50.9, respectively. Infant mortality rates are telling indicators of the state of a country's healthcare system and level of provision. Africa dominates the list of countries with the highest infant mortality rate.

COUNTRIES WITH LOWEST INFANT MORTALITY RATE

Deaths per 1,000 live births

1	Japan	3.3
2	Sweden	3.4
3	Iceland	3.5
4	Singapore	3.6
5	Finland	3.7
6	Norway	3.9
7	Andorra	4.1
8	Germany	4.2
9	Netherlands	4.3
10	Austria	4.3

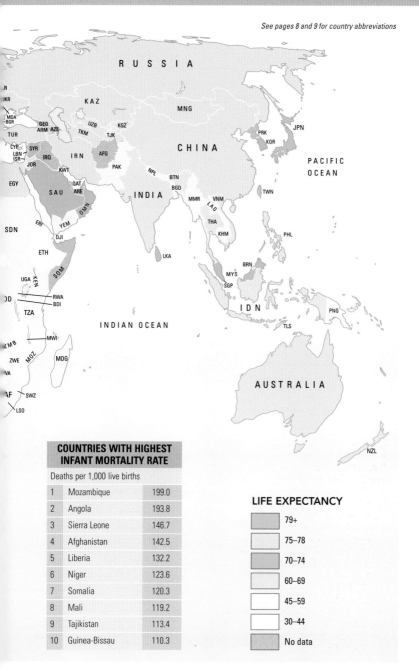

See pages 8 and 9 for country abbreviations

COUNTRIES WITH HIGHEST INFANT MORTALITY RATE

Deaths per 1,000 live births

1	Mozambique	199.0
2	Angola	193.8
3	Sierra Leone	146.7
4	Afghanistan	142.5
5	Liberia	132.2
6	Niger	123.6
7	Somalia	120.3
8	Mali	119.2
9	Tajikistan	113.4
10	Guinea-Bissau	110.3

LIFE EXPECTANCY

	79+
	75–78
	70–74
	60–69
	45–59
	30–44
	No data

95

DISEASE

Disease control made great advances in the last half of the 20th century, but many problems remain. Some microorganisms have become resistant to antibiotics, like penicillin. Some nearly eradicated diseases have returned, with Europe in 2002 reporting 472,000 cases of tuberculosis that caused 73,000 deaths. Global TB cases rose to about 8.8 million with 1.8 million deaths. New diseases have appeared, such as legionnaire's disease and the Ebola virus in 1976 and AIDS in 1979. By 2003, AIDS had caused some 25 million deaths, and Ebola deaths totaled about 1,200. Other diseases reported worldwide in 2002 included 586 million cases of measles, 18.7 million cases of tetanus, 9.2 million of diphtheria, 1.9 million of polio and 705,000 of yellow fever.

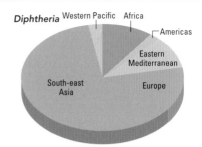

Diphtheria

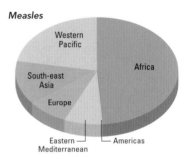

Measles

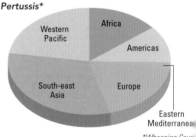

*Pertussis**

*Whooping Cough

IMMUNIZATION

Percentage of target population vaccinated, by antigen

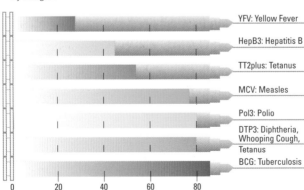

YFV: Yellow Fever

HepB3: Hepatitis B

TT2plus: Tetanus

MCV: Measles

Pol3: Polio

DTP3: Diphtheria, Whooping Cough, Tetanus

BCG: Tuberculosis

◀ The colored part of each needle represents the percentage vaccinated with antigen, which is a substance, normally a toxin, that stimulates the production of antibodies.

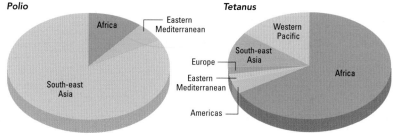

Polio

Africa
Eastern Mediterranean
South-east Asia

Tetanus

Western Pacific
South-east Asia
Europe
Eastern Mediterranean
Americas
Africa

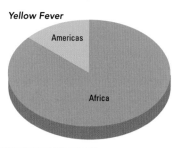

Yellow Fever

Americas
Africa

REPORTED CASES OF MAJOR DISEASE PER REGION

◄ *Each pie chart shows either Africa or Southeast Asia reporting the most cases of a disease.*

▼ *The poorer health in developing countries is reflected in the years lost to ill health. In many cases, these are double the European rate.*

MOST YEARS LOST TO ILL HEALTH (MEN)

	% of total life expectancy	years
Yemen	18.4	10.8
Iraq	17.5	10.3
Angola	16.6	6.3
Liberia	16.1	6.5
Somalia	16.1	6.9
Niger	15.9	6.8
Sierra Leone	15.9	5.1
Afghanistan	15.8	6.6
Iran	15.7	10.4
Kiribati	15.4	9.5

MOST YEARS LOST TO ILL HEALTH (WOMEN)

	% of total life expectancy	years
Yemen	18.5	11.5
Iraq	18.4	11.6
Somalia	17.7	8.1
Afghanistan	17.7	7.7
Niger	17.5	7.5
Iran	17.5	12.5
Kiribati	16.5	11.0
Angola	16.4	6.9
Morocco	16.4	11.9
Laos	16.4	9.2

LEAST YEARS LOST TO ILL HEALTH (MEN)

	% of total life expectancy	years
Germany	7.8	5.9
Italy	7.8	6.0
Japan	7.8	6.1
Norway	7.8	5.9
Sweden	7.9	6.2
Finland	8.1	6.1
Iceland	8.1	6.3
Malta	8.1	6.2
San Marino	8.2	6.3
Spain	8.2	6.2

LEAST YEARS LOST TO ILL HEALTH (WOMEN)

	% of total life expectancy	years
Japan	8.8	7.5
Spain	9.3	7.7
Germany	9.3	7.6
Sweden	9.5	7.9
Italy	9.5	7.8
San Marino	9.6	8.1
Switzerland	9.7	8.1
Luxembourg	9.8	8.0
Finland	9.9	8.0
Norway	9.9	8.1

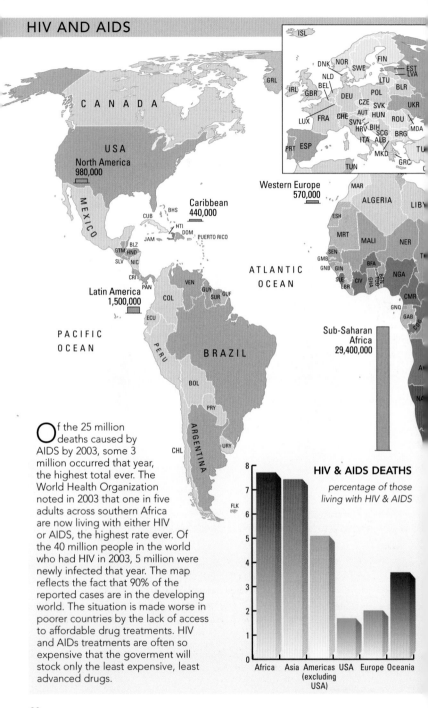

ISL

DNK NOR SWE FIN
NLD EST
IRL GBR BEL DEU POL LTU LVA
LUX FRA CZE SVK UKR
CHE AUT HUN
SVN HRV BIH ROU MDA
PRT ESP ITA SCG BRG
ALB TU
MKD
TUN GRC

GRL

C A N A D A

U S A
North America
980,000

Western Europe
570,000

MAR
ALGERIA LIBY

ESH

MRT MALI NER

SEN T
GMB BFA
GNB GIN NGA
SLE CIV BEN
LBR GHA TGO
CMR
GNQ
GAB CO

CUB BHS
HTI
DOM
JAM PUERTO RICO

Caribbean
440,000

ATLANTIC
OCEAN

BLZ
GTM HND
SLV NIC
CRI PAN

Latin America
1,500,000

VEN
GUY SUR GUF
COL

ECU

PACIFIC
OCEAN

PERU
BRAZIL

Sub-Saharan
Africa
29,400,000

BOL

PRY

A

NA

CHL URY

ARGENTINA

FLK

Of the 25 million deaths caused by AIDS by 2003, some 3 million occurred that year, the highest total ever. The World Health Organization noted in 2003 that one in five adults across southern Africa are now living with either HIV or AIDS, the highest rate ever. Of the 40 million people in the world who had HIV in 2003, 5 million were newly infected that year. The map reflects the fact that 90% of the reported cases are in the developing world. The situation is made worse in poorer countries by the lack of access to affordable drug treatments. HIV and AIDs treatments are often so expensive that the goverment will stock only the least expensive, least advanced drugs.

HIV & AIDS DEATHS

percentage of those living with HIV & AIDS

(bar chart with y-axis from 0 to 8; categories: Africa, Asia, Americas (excluding USA), USA, Europe, Oceania)

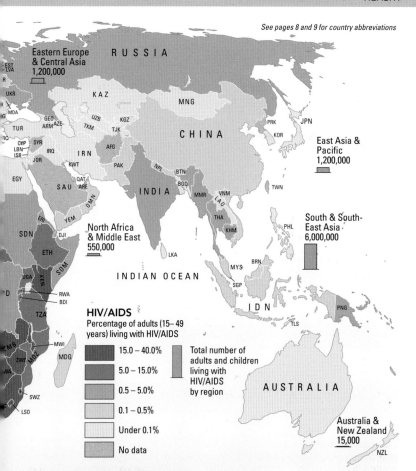

See pages 8 and 9 for country abbreviations

Eastern Europe
& Central Asia
1,200,000

RUSSIA

KAZ

MNG

CHINA

East Asia &
Pacific
1,200,000

North Africa
& Middle East
550,000

INDIA

South & South-
East Asia
6,000,000

INDIAN OCEAN

HIV/AIDS
Percentage of adults (15–49
years) living with HIV/AIDS

	15.0 – 40.0%
	5.0 – 15.0%
	0.5 – 5.0%
	0.1 – 0.5%
	Under 0.1%
	No data

Total number of
adults and children
living with
HIV/AIDS
by region

AUSTRALIA

Australia &
New Zealand
15,000

EPIDEMIC UPDATE		
Number of people living with HIV/AIDS	**40 million**	**(34–46 million)**
Adults	37 million	(31–43 million)
Children under 15 years	2.5 million	(2.1–2.9 million)
People newly infected with HIV in 2003	**5 million**	**(4.2–5.8 million)**
Adults	4.2 million	(3.6–4.8 million)
Children under 15 years	700,000	(590,000–810,000)
AIDS deaths in 2003	**3 million**	**(2.5–3.5 million)**
Adults	2.5 million	(2.1–2.9 million)
Children under 15 years	500,000	(420,000–580,000)

*The ranges around the estimates in this table define the boundaries within
which the actual numbers lie, based on the best available information.*

*Each day in 2003, an
estimated 14,000
people were newly
infected with HIV,
according to the
World Health
Organization. It has
warned that Eastern
Europe and Central
Asia could become
the newest regions to
experience serious HIV
and AIDS epidemics.*

SMOKING AND ALCOHOL

Tobacco and alcohol consumption are major causes of deaths around the world. About 1.3 billion people used tobacco in 2004, and this was expected to rise to 1.7 billion by 2025. About 84% of the smokers live in developing countries. The World Health Organization estimates that tobacco use kills 4.9 million people every year and this should double in the next 20 years. A person dies from a tobacco-related illness every 6.5 seconds. High-income nations spend between 6% and 15% on health care costs to treat tobacco related diseases, according to the World Bank. Egypt estimated its 2003 health costs from smoking were US$545.5 million, and China in the mid1990s estimated US$6.5 billion.

SMOKERS
Cigarettes smoked per adult annually

- 3,001 to 4,000
- 2,001 to 3,000
- 1,001 to 2,000
- 501 to 1,000
- 100 to 500
- No data

Countries with highest percentage of smokers

Country	Percentage
Namibia	50.0%
Kenya	49.4%
Bosnia-Herzegovina	48.0%
Serbia & Montenegro	47.0%
Mongolia	46.7%
Yemen	44.5%
Turkey	44.0%
Romania	43.5%
Slovak Republic	42.6%
Lebanon	40.5%

0   10   20   30   40   50

COUNTRIES WITH THE LOWEST PERCENTAGE OF SMOKERS

	Country	Percentage
1	Libya	4.0%
2	Senegal	4.6%
3	Rwanda	5.5%
4	Oman	8.5%
5	Nigeria	8.6%
6	United Arab Emirates	9.0%
7	Haiti	9.7%
8	Bahamas	11.5%
9	Saudi Arabia	11.5%
10	Sudan	12.9%

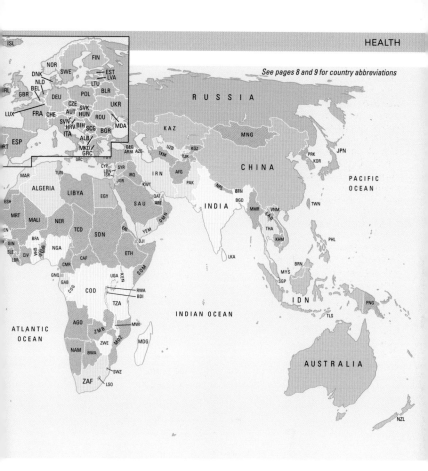

See pages 8 and 9 for country abbreviations

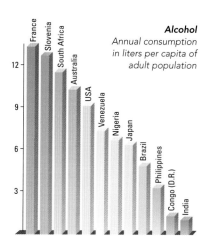

Alcohol
*Annual consumption
in liters per capita of
adult population*

◀ ALCOHOL

*This bar graph shows the wide variety of
nations with high alcohol consumption.
Global consumption has grown in recent
decades because of an increase in
developing nations. The World Health
Organization estimates that 140 million
people suffer from alcohol dependence,
and alcohol consumption causes nearly 2
million deaths each year. It is a cause of
oesophageal cancer, liver disease, motor
vehicle accidents and violent acts.*

SAFE WATER

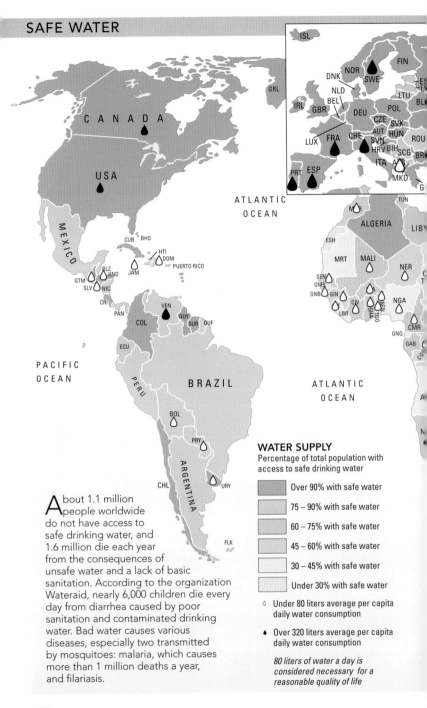

About 1.1 million people worldwide do not have access to safe drinking water, and 1.6 million die each year from the consequences of unsafe water and a lack of basic sanitation. According to the organization Wateraid, nearly 6,000 children die every day from diarrhea caused by poor sanitation and contaminated drinking water. Bad water causes various diseases, especially two transmitted by mosquitoes: malaria, which causes more than 1 million deaths a year, and filariasis.

WATER SUPPLY
Percentage of total population with access to safe drinking water

Over 90% with safe water

75 – 90% with safe water

60 – 75% with safe water

45 – 60% with safe water

30 – 45% with safe water

Under 30% with safe water

◇ Under 80 liters average per capita daily water consumption

◆ Over 320 liters average per capita daily water consumption

80 liters of water a day is considered necessary for a reasonable quality of life

See pages 8 and 9 for country abbreviations

LEAST WELL-PROVIDED COUNTRIES	
Afghanistan	13%
Ethiopia	24%
Chad	27%
Sierra Leone	28%
Cambodia	30%
Mauritania	37%
Angola	38%
Oman	39%

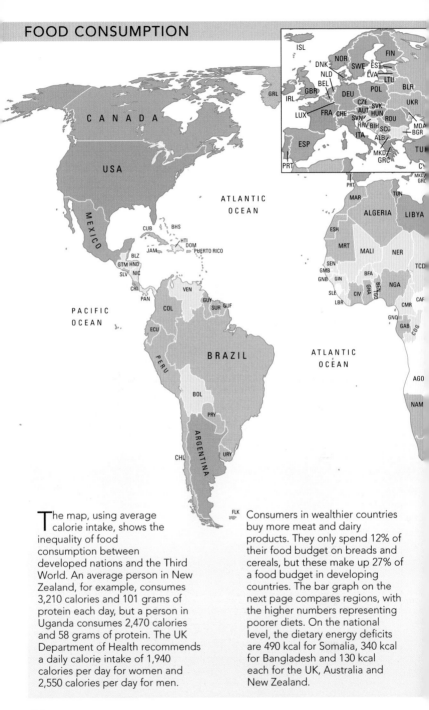

The map, using average calorie intake, shows the inequality of food consumption between developed nations and the Third World. An average person in New Zealand, for example, consumes 3,210 calories and 101 grams of protein each day, but a person in Uganda consumes 2,470 calories and 58 grams of protein. The UK Department of Health recommends a daily calorie intake of 1,940 calories per day for women and 2,550 calories per day for men.

Consumers in wealthier countries buy more meat and dairy products. They only spend 12% of their food budget on breads and cereals, but these make up 27% of a food budget in developing countries. The bar graph on the next page compares regions, with the higher numbers representing poorer diets. On the national level, the dietary energy deficits are 490 kcal for Somalia, 340 kcal for Bangladesh and 130 kcal each for the UK, Australia and New Zealand.

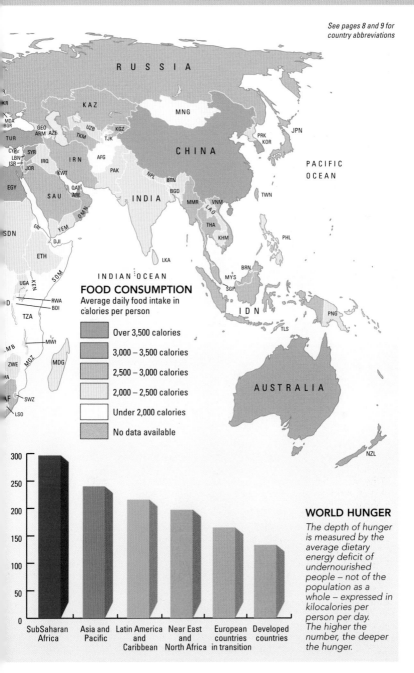

See pages 8 and 9 for country abbreviations

FOOD CONSUMPTION

Average daily food intake in calories per person

- Over 3,500 calories
- 3,000 – 3,500 calories
- 2,500 – 3,000 calories
- 2,000 – 2,500 calories
- Under 2,000 calories
- No data available

WORLD HUNGER

The depth of hunger is measured by the average dietary energy deficit of undernourished people – not of the population as a whole – expressed in kilocalories per person per day. The higher the number, the deeper the hunger.

(Chart categories: SubSaharan Africa; Asia and Pacific; Latin America and Caribbean; Near East and North Africa; European countries in transition; Developed countries)

Children and Education

Quality of Education
Primary and Secondary Education
Tertiary Education
Child Rights

Dramatic progress in education occurred in the 20th century, as access to a basic free education was opened to women and minorities throughout the world. More improvement is needed in some regions, however, to improve the quality of education and, especially in Arab states, to provide equal opportunities for women. Poverty and child labor are further hinderance to the basic right to education, with millions of children denied schooling because they are forced to work. The resulting illiteracy hinders a person's productivity and the opportunities for self-employment and a better life.

QUALITY OF EDUCATION

The opportunity to attend school is a basic human right and should be made available to all children. It is the job of their government to provide a quality education. This was emphasized in 2000 by the UNESCO World Education Forum meeting in Dakar, Senegal. In some countries, minorities and women still receive no education or a poorer one. Separate schools for races was a proven failure in South Africa and the USA. The US Supreme Court in 1954 ended the segregated 'separate but equal' schools that offered a good education for whites but not blacks. The map, based on UNESCO figures, shows the relative importance that nations give to education. Richer countries can afford to spend a smaller percentage of their higher gross domestic product (GDP) to provide a quality education.

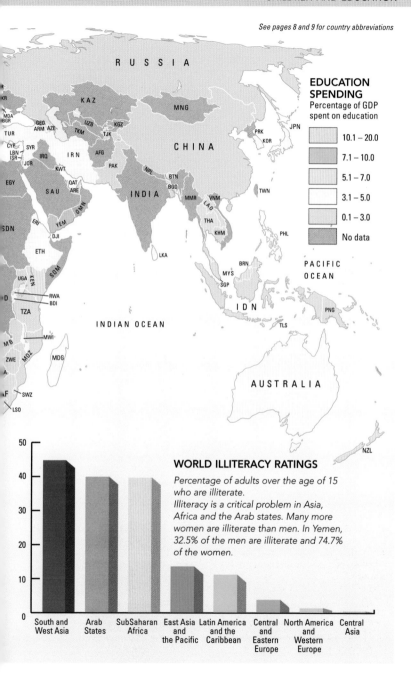

See pages 8 and 9 for country abbreviations

EDUCATION SPENDING
Percentage of GDP spent on education

	10.1 – 20.0
	7.1 – 10.0
	5.1 – 7.0
	3.1 – 5.0
	0.1 – 3.0
	No data

PACIFIC OCEAN

INDIAN OCEAN

AUSTRALIA

WORLD ILLITERACY RATINGS

Percentage of adults over the age of 15 who are illiterate.
Illiteracy is a critical problem in Asia, Africa and the Arab states. Many more women are illiterate than men. In Yemen, 32.5% of the men are illiterate and 74.7% of the women.

Chart categories (x-axis): South and West Asia; Arab States; SubSaharan Africa; East Asia and the Pacific; Latin America and the Caribbean; Central and Eastern Europe; North America and Western Europe; Central Asia

109

PRIMARY AND SECONDARY EDUCATION

Good primary schooling is vital to a child's development. Research in the Third World shows that substantial benefits are gained by only five or six years of formal education. These gains include better wages, productivity, health, as well as more meaning and value to lives. The rewards are further increased by a seondary education, but many countries need to provide better access. In Arab states, 40% of the population of high school age (about 12 to 18 years) do not attend school. This map shows the high attendance figures for Western Europe, North America, Australia, New Zealand and Kazakhstan.

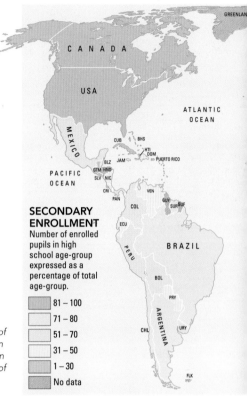

SECONDARY ENROLLMENT
Number of enrolled pupils in high school age-group expressed as a percentage of total age-group.

- 81 – 100
- 71 – 80
- 51 – 70
- 31 – 50
- 1 – 30
- No data

▼ **PRIMARY ENROLLMENT**
Africa lags behind on the numbers of children of elementary-school age in school. In 2000, the World Education Forum set a target that all children of kindergarten age would have free schooling by 2015.

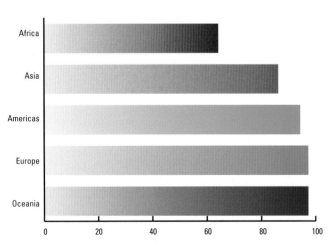

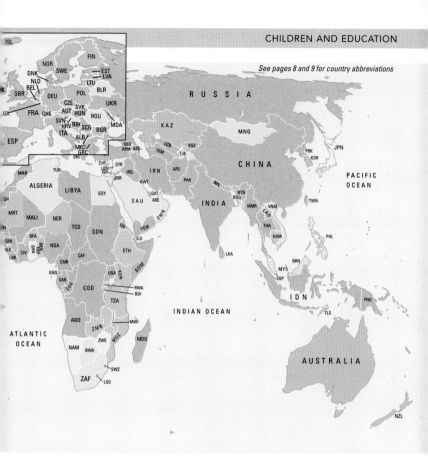

See pages 8 and 9 for country abbreviations

▼ SIZE OF CLASSES
High school pupil to teacher ratio

A key indicator of the quality of an education is the number of students in a classroom. The higher the ratio, the less individual attention a pupil receives.

LOWEST RATIO OF PUPILS PER TEACHER	
Bermuda	7
Lebanon	7
Qatar	7
Azerbaijan	8
Israel	8
Spain	8
Belarus	9
Greece	9
Turks and Caicos Islands	9
Cayman Islands	10

HIGHEST RATIO OF PUPILS PER TEACHER	
Eritrea	52
Bangladesh	38
Malawi	38
Philippines	36
Bhutan	33
Nicaragua	32
Burkina Faso	31
Togo	31
Nepal	30
South Africa	29

Tertiary, or higher, education produces a nation's professionals, such as scientists, engineers, doctors, lawyers and politicians. As the map shows, countries with the highest percentage of students in tertiary education include the USA, Russia, Australia and New Zealand. Western European nations also educate a large percentage. In 2000–2001, there were 13,595,580 students in tertiary education in the USA, 12,143,723 in China, 2,067,349 in the UK and 845,132 in Australia. The USA was among those wealthier nations to popularize the idea that most students should consider a university education, but the country's average annual tuition fees in 2001–2002 were $3,746 for a four-year state school and $16,287 for a private one. Such costs and the daunting prospect of debt upon graduation means that higher education remains a luxury in many countries. Meanwhile, the push for improved facilities and comparable international standards has left many institutions in need of financial aid. Debate continued in Britain in 2004, as the government supported rises in university student numbers and also tuition fees.

See pages 8 and 9 for country abbreviations

TERTIARY ENROLLMENT

Number of pupils enrolled in higher education as percentage of official age-group

- 61 – 80
- 51 – 60
- 31 – 50
- 16 – 30
- 1 – 15
- No data

LOWEST PROPORTION OF FEMALE STUDENTS	
Congo	11.9%
Eritrea	13.4%
Mauritania	16.8%
Netherlands	20.0%
Ethiopia	21.4%
Tajikistan	23.9%
Tanzania	23.9%
Niger	24.8%
Burundi	27.2%
Ghana	28.5%

HIGHEST PROPORTION OF FEMALE STUDENTS	
Turks and Caicos Islands	75.0%
Cayman Islands	74.6%
Qatar	73.2%
Barbados	70.6%
Jamaica	65.0%
Brunei	64.8%
Uruguay	64.0%
Lesotho	63.5%
Palau	63.5%
Namibia	63.4%

◄ **FEMALE UNIVERSITY STUDENTS**

This interesting list finds Arab and African countries with higher percentages of female students than those countries traditionally considered to be more 'developed'.

113

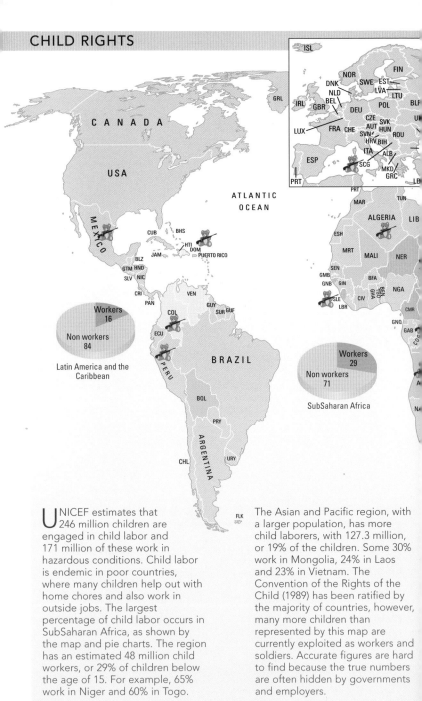

Workers
16

Non workers
84

Latin America and the
Caribbean

Workers
29

Non workers
71

SubSaharan Africa

UNICEF estimates that
246 million children are
engaged in child labor and
171 million of these work in
hazardous conditions. Child labor
is endemic in poor countries,
where many children help out with
home chores and also work in
outside jobs. The largest
percentage of child labor occurs in
SubSaharan Africa, as shown by
the map and pie charts. The region
has an estimated 48 million child
workers, or 29% of children below
the age of 15. For example, 65%
work in Niger and 60% in Togo.

The Asian and Pacific region, with
a larger population, has more
child laborers, with 127.3 million,
or 19% of the children. Some 30%
work in Mongolia, 24% in Laos
and 23% in Vietnam. The
Convention of the Rights of the
Child (1989) has been ratified by
the majority of countries, however,
many more children than
represented by this map are
currently exploited as workers and
soldiers. Accurate figures are hard
to find because the true numbers
are often hidden by governments
and employers.

See pages 8 and 9 for country abbreviations

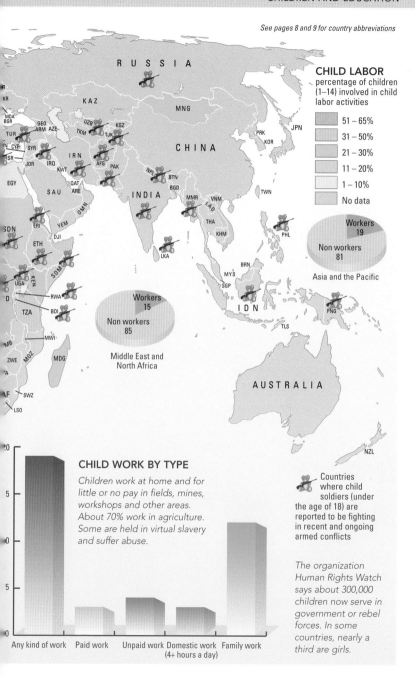

CHILD LABOR
percentage of children
(1–14) involved in child
labor activities

51 – 65%

31 – 50%

21 – 30%

11 – 20%

1 – 10%

No data

Workers
19

Non workers
81

Asia and the Pacific

Workers
15

Non workers
85

Middle East and
North Africa

CHILD WORK BY TYPE

*Children work at home and for
little or no pay in fields, mines,
workshops and other areas.
About 70% work in agriculture.
Some are held in virtual slavery
and suffer abuse.*

Any kind of work   Paid work   Unpaid work   Domestic work   Family work
(4+ hours a day)

Countries
where child
soldiers (under
the age of 18) are
reported to be fighting
in recent and ongoing
armed conflicts

*The organization
Human Rights Watch
says about 300,000
children now serve in
government or rebel
forces. In some
countries, nearly a
third are girls.*

115

Wealth

The world is divided by the inequality of wealth. The major developed nations encouraged the policy of providing aid to poor countries to help in their development. However, due to severe macroeconomic crises during the 1970s there were serious setbacks in the development of many African and Latin American countries. Many were caught in a debt trap (being forced to take out more loans to fund repayment of previous loans). Further economic globalization, while benefiting some, has often led to greater inequality and impoverishment of many in developing countries. The economic problems of wealthy nations are small by comparison, but jobs can be lost and life styles lowered by the soaring prices of houses, oil, food and other essentials. For this reason, governments strive to control inflation to maintain a healthy economy.

GROSS DOMESTIC PRODUCT (GDP)

A nation's gross domestic product (GDP) measures its total goods and services produced annually, and this indicates the strength of its industry. The map shows the GDP per person in US dollars, with Europe, North America and Australia in the top level. In 2003, the major Western nations had a GDP of US$23,363. Regional averages included Latin America and the Caribbean with US$7,050, the Arab states with US$5,038, South Asia with US$2,730 and SubSaharan Africa with US$1,830. Developing countries averaged US$3,850, and those with large populations have small GDPs despite experiencing a rapid growth in goods (China) or services (India).

GDP PER CAPITA
PPP US$

	20,001 – 54,000
	9,001 – 20,000
	5,001 – 9,000
	2,001 – 5,000
	1 – 2,000
	No data

▶ *These 2003 figures from the United Nations Human Development Index show the great disparity between 'have' and 'have not' nations. Not listed are Australia with US$25,370, Germany with US$25,350, the UK with US$24,160, France with US$23,990, Kuwait with US$18,700 and Russia with US$7,100.*

LOWEST GDP PER CAPITA		HIGHEST GDP PER CAPITA	
Sierra Leone	470	Luxembourg	53,780
Tanzania	520	USA	34,320
Malawi	570	Ireland	32,410
Congo (Dem. Rep. of the)	680	Iceland	29,990
Burundi	690	Norfolk Island	29,620
Zambia	780	Denmark	29,000
Yemen	790	Switzerland	28,100
Ethiopia	810	Netherlands	27,190
Mali	810	Canada	27,130
Madagascar	830	Austria	26,730

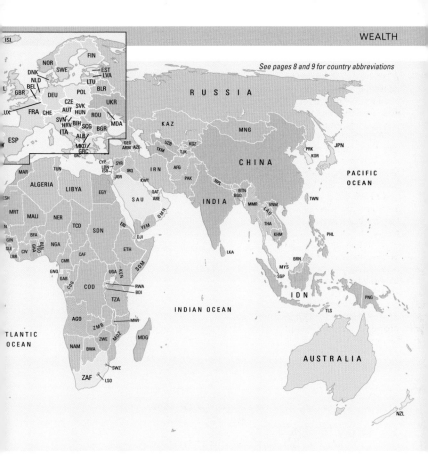

See pages 8 and 9 for country abbreviations

▼ GDP AVERAGE ANNUAL GROWTH

*Figures given as percentages (1990–2001)
The GDP average annual growth rate can
increase faster for a developing country
than one that already has a strong GDP.*

*Thus, China's grew at 9.7% and India's at
5.8% compared with the UK's of 2.6%.
Russia, with economic turmoil during this
period, recorded a falling GDP of –2.7%.*

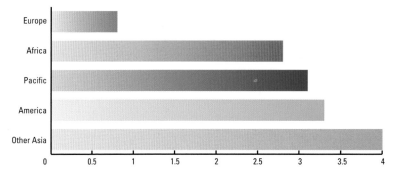

INCOME AND THE WEALTH GAP

Little has been done to close the wide income gap between wealthy and poor nations. In fact income equality has been increasing. Companies in developed nations have recently increased the outsourcing of production and services to the Third World. This has created much needed jobs, but the workers are poorly paid – the major reason that developed nations use foreign labor.

▼ **The Wealth Gap** *The world's richest and poorest countries, by Gross National Income per capita in US$.*

TOP 5 COUNTRIES	
Luxembourg	$42,060
Switzerland	$38,140
Japan	$35,620
Norway	$34,530
Bermuda	$34,470

BOTTOM 5 COUNTRIES	
Ethiopia	$100
Burundi	$110
Sierra Leone	$130
Eritrea	$170
Malawi	$170

GNI per capita is calculated by dividing a country's Gross National Income by its total population.

▶ **Indicators** *The gap between the world's rich and poor is now so great that it is difficult to illustrate on a single graph. Within each income group (as defined by the World Bank), however, comparisons have some meaning. The wealth gap in many developing countries, though, is wide, with a small, rich class and a large, impoverished majority, while many high-income countries contain an underclass of unemployed and homeless people.*

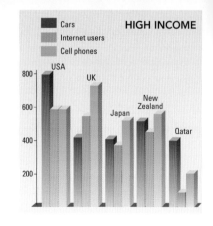

- Cars
- Internet users
- Cell phones

HIGH INCOME

USA
UK
New Zealand
Japan
Qatar

See pages 8 and 9 for country abbreviations

LEVELS OF INCOME

Gross National Income per capita: the value of total production divided by the population

Over 400% of world average

200 – 400%

100 – 200%

(World average wealth per person US$4,890)

50 – 100%

25 – 50%

10 – 25%

Under 10%

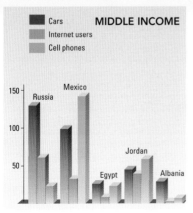

MIDDLE INCOME

- Cars
- Internet users
- Cell phones

Russia Mexico

150

100

Jordan

50

Egypt Albania

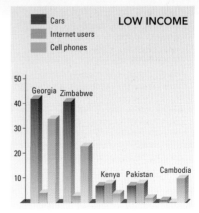

LOW INCOME

- Cars
- Internet users
- Cell phones

50

Georgia Zimbabwe

40

30

20

Kenya Pakistan Cambodia

10

The map indicates that most of the world's countries kept inflation within 1–7.5% in 2000. Many factors can cause inflation to rise, such as economic growth that encourages higher consumer prices. The consumer price index is used to measure inflation. When the US economy began to recover in early 2004, prices rose 4.4%, compared to only 1.9% throughout 2003. China's inflation hit a seven-year high in 2004 following higher food costs. Governments can cool inflation by raising interest rates. Inflation can have disastrous consequences for a nation's economy. Inflation commonly occurs in times of crisis, for example war, when a government is forced to increase the amount of paper money in circulation. After World War I, Germans found their life's savings wiped out by inflation caused by the sudden flood of paper money, the effects of which contributed to the downfall of the government.

See pages 8 and 9 for country abbreviations

HIGHEST AVERAGE INFLATION	
Congo (Dem. Rep.)	1423%
Angola	740%
Turkmenistan	407%

LOWEST AVERAGE INFLATION	
Antigua and Barbuda	−11.5%
Argentina*	−3.1%
Bahrain	−0.1%

* During 2002, Argentina experienced a sharp rise in inflation which is not reflected on this map.

INFLATION
Average annual rate of inflation

- Over 50%
- 20 – 50%
- 7.5 – 20%
- 1 – 7.5%
- Negative inflation
- No data available

AID AND DEBT

Developing nations receive financial aid from richer countries, but most of this involves loans from the World Bank's International Development Association and private banks. The 42 poorest countries owed US$205 billion in 2003. Although loans can be interest free with 30 years to repay, poor countries struggle under the burden.

World leaders promised in 2000 to write off over $100 billion of these debts, but most of this relief has been delayed by their governments. Debt repayments distorts the priorities of poor countries as they have to cut down their investment in other areas including education, health and welfare.

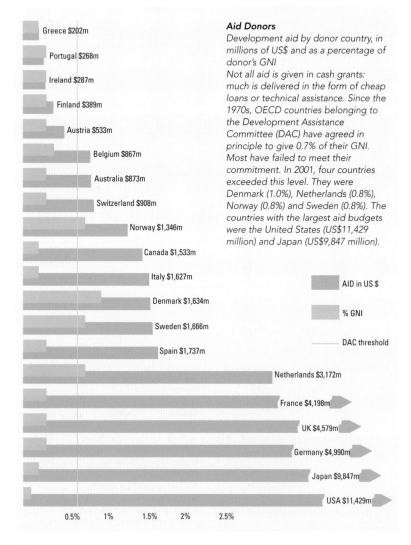

Greece $202m

Portugal $268m

Ireland $287m

Finland $389m

Austria $533m

Belgium $867m

Australia $873m

Switzerland $908m

Norway $1,346m

Canada $1,533m

Italy $1,627m

Denmark $1,634m

Sweden $1,666m

Spain $1,737m

Netherlands $3,172m

France $4,198m

UK $4,579m

Germany $4,990m

Japan $9,847m

USA $11,429m

0.5%   1%   1.5%   2%   2.5%

Aid Donors
Development aid by donor country, in millions of US$ and as a percentage of donor's GNI
Not all aid is given in cash grants: much is delivered in the form of cheap loans or technical assistance. Since the 1970s, OECD countries belonging to the Development Assistance Committee (DAC) have agreed in principle to give 0.7% of their GNI. Most have failed to meet their commitment. In 2001, four countries exceeded this level. They were Denmark (1.0%), Netherlands (0.8%), Norway (0.8%) and Sweden (0.8%). The countries with the largest aid budgets were the United States (US$11,429 million) and Japan (US$9,847 million).

AID in US $

% GNI

DAC threshold

EXTERNAL DEBT BY COUNTRIES' INCOME
US$millions

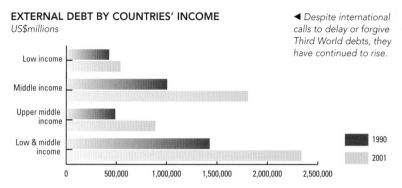

◀ *Despite international calls to delay or forgive Third World debts, they have continued to rise.*

1990
2001

TOTAL EXTERNAL DEBT
US$millions

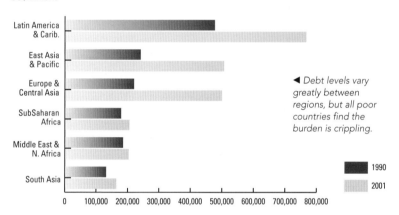

◀ *Debt levels vary greatly between regions, but all poor countries find the burden is crippling.*

1990
2001

SEVERELY INDEBTED – TOP TEN	
Value of debt as % of GNI	
Liberia	435.6
Sao Tome & Principe	238.8
Guinea-Bissau	231.5
Congo, Dem Rep	222.4
Congo	220.8
Mauritania	143.0
Guyana	138.3
Angola	118.9
Zambia	115.3
Sierra Leone	114.4

Nine of the ten worst indebted nations on this list are in Africa. Their debt relief reached US$43 billion in 2003, but more is urgently needed. In 2002, the World Bank calculated Algeria's total external debt to be US$22,800 million. Interest and principal repayments were 20.8% of all export revenues. The continent suffers from civil wars, adverse weather conditions, the rapid spread of HIV and AIDS, exploitative multinational corporations, external interventions and low economic growth rates. African nations also encounter trade protectionism in richer countries. Although foreign investment is increasing, most goes to South Africa and oil-exporting countries.

125

Trade and Industry

All modern nations depend upon international trade to sustain a healthy economy. The export of manufactured goods creates jobs, and these are often made secure by protective tariffs on imports. A recent trend in wealthy countries has been the out-sourcing of manufacturing and services to Third World countries, a development that costs jobs but raises company profits in the west. Another significant shift in the latter part of the 20th century has been the growing economic power of East Asia, led by such countries as Japan, South Korea and China.

WORLD TRADE

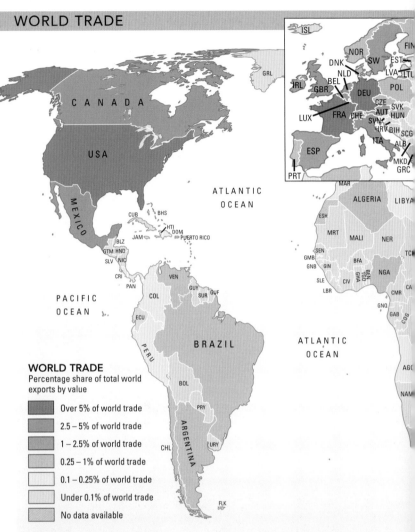

WORLD TRADE
Percentage share of total world exports by value

- Over 5% of world trade
- 2.5 – 5% of world trade
- 1 – 2.5% of world trade
- 0.25 – 1% of world trade
- 0.1 – 0.25% of world trade
- Under 0.1% of world trade
- No data available

The map shows the trading strength of countries, but does not indicate recent trends. China is rapidly emerging as a world trading power, following an increase in private companies and the acquisition of Hong Kong. World agreements have made trade freer within regions. Examples include the European Union (EU) and the North American Free Trade Agreement (NAFTA). The World Trade Organization (WTO) regulates international trade. It was established by the United Nations in 1995 to replace the General Agreement on Tariffs and Trade (GATT). Not everyone is happy with the way such organizations have opened up world trade and debate continues as to the effect international competition could have on smaller economies and on unfairness of trade practices of developed countries.

See pages 8 and 9 for country abbreviations

THE MAIN TRADING NATIONS

The imports and exports of the top ten trading nations as a percentage of world trade. Each country's trade in manufactured goods is shown in dark blue. The total trade is shown in light blue.

Imports / Exports

USA
Germany
Japan
UK
France
China
Italy
Canada
Netherlands
Mexico

129

Manufactured goods make up the vast majority of global exported and imported products. In 2002, the USA exported US$554.9 billion and imported US$974.6 billion of manufactured goods. Its three largest exports were electrical machinery, vehicles and power-generating machinery, while the major imports were motor vehicles, electrical machinery and automatic data processing equipment/office machinery. As noted on the map, manufactured goods dominate the export figures of countries that offer cheap labor, such as China, Mexico and Eastern Europe. This, in turn, has devastated certain industries in more wealthy nations, such as the steel and shipbuilding industries in Britain. It also creates trade imbalances: the US trade deficit reached a record US$489.4 billion in 2003.

See pages 8 and 9 for country abbreviations

MOST RELIANT ON EXPORTS

Countries most dependent on the export of manufactured goods

Malta	91%
Bangladesh	90%
China	90%
Japan	88%
South Korea	83%
Luxembourg	83%
Pakistan	83%

INDUSTRY AND TRADE

Manufactured goods (including machinery and transportation) as a percentage of total exports

- Over 75%
- 50 – 75%
- 25 – 50%
- 10 – 25%
- Under 10%

131

DEPENDENCE ON TRADE

In today's shrinking world, the economic health of virtually all nations is dependent on trade. Nearly a quarter of Mexico's gross domestic product (GDP) and about 40% of Canada's Gross National Product (GNP) depend on exports to the United States. On the pie charts below, no developing country is named as a major exporter, and many are heavily dependent on trade preferences and access to markets in the European Union (EU) and USA. The latter's Andean Trade Preference Act, for example, gives duty-free access to the US market to Bolivia, Colombia, Ecuador and Peru. For a few countries, such as China, the USA requires a presidential waiver for normal trade relations, with human rights conditions attached.

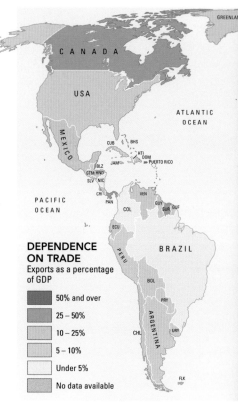

DEPENDENCE ON TRADE
Exports as a percentage of GDP

- 50% and over
- 25 – 50%
- 10 – 25%
- 5 – 10%
- Under 5%
- No data available

MAJOR EXPORTS
Leading manufactured items and their exporters.

Motor Vehicles
World total: US$299,334 million

Germany 20%
Japan 19%
Canada 12%
France 7%
Spain 6%
Belgium 6%
Mexico 5%
USA 5%
UK 5%
South Korea 4%
Italy 2%
Other 10%

Telecommunication Gear
World total: US$214,456 million

USA 12%
UK 8%
Japan 8%
Germany 7%
China 6%
France 6%
Sweden 6%
Canada 5%
Mexico 5%
Other 39%

USA 17%
Singapore 11%
Netherlands 8%
Japan 8%
UK 8%
China 6%
South Korea 5%
Mexico 5%
Other 33%

Computers
World total: US$182,866 million

132

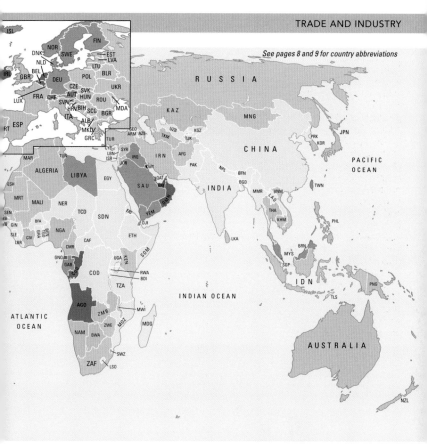

See pages 8 and 9 for country abbreviations

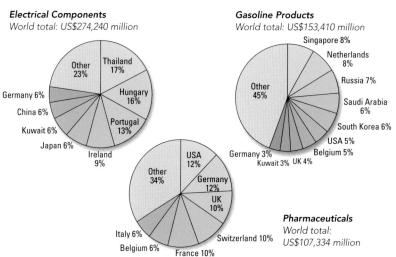

Electrical Components
World total: US$274,240 million

- Thailand 17%
- Hungary 16%
- Portugal 13%
- Ireland 9%
- Japan 6%
- Kuwait 6%
- China 6%
- Germany 6%
- Other 23%

Gasoline Products
World total: US$153,410 million

- Singapore 8%
- Netherlands 8%
- Russia 7%
- Saudi Arabia 6%
- South Korea 6%
- USA 5%
- Belgium 5%
- UK 4%
- Kuwait 3%
- Germany 3%
- Other 45%

Pharmaceuticals
World total: US$107,334 million

- USA 12%
- Germany 12%
- UK 10%
- Switzerland 10%
- France 10%
- Belgium 6%
- Italy 6%
- Other 34%

Many jobs depend upon exports. In Canada, approximately one in every five jobs relies on the export industry. Not all workers profit from exports, but the success of a nation's trade can be seen on this map highlighting the value of a country's exports per person. In this way, the size of the export industry is made relative to the size of the population. Despite China's dominance of much of the export market, the comparative size of the population negates much of the economic impact at individual level.

Agriculture is an important export product for many countries. Australia exports some 80% of the gross value of its agriculture, although crops can be grown on only 6% of the land. They include wheat, barley, sugarcane and fruits. US farmers are also dependent on exports, which include one of every five rows of corn. Other major US exports are soybeans, vegetables, fruits and wheat.

See pages 8 and 9 for
country abbreviations

RUSSIA

KAZ

MNG

CHINA

JPN
PRK
KOR

PACIFIC
OCEAN

TWN

EST
LVA

UKR

MDA

GEO
ARM AZE
TUR

CYP
LBN
ISR

SYR
JOR
IRQ

KWT

QAT
ARE

OMAN

YEM

UZB
TKM
TJK

KGZ

AFG

IRN

PAK

NPL

BTN

BGD

INDIA

MMR

VNM
LAO

THA

KHM

PHL

BRN

MYS
SGP

EGY

SAU

ERI

SDN

ETH

DJI

SOM

UGA KEN

COD

RWA
BDI

TZA

ZMB

MWI

ZWE

WA

MOZ

MDG

SWZ

LSO

AF

LKA

INDIAN OCEAN

IDN

TLS

PNG

AUSTRALIA

NZL

EXPORTS PER CAPITA

Value of exports in US$ divided by
total population

- Over 10,000
- 5,000 – 10,000
- 1,000 – 5,000
- 500 – 1,000
- 100 – 500
- Under 100

HIGHEST PER CAPITA	
Kuwait	113,614
Liechtenstein	78,848
Singapore	31,860
Aruba	31,429
Hong Kong	28,290

LOWEST PER CAPITA	
Afghanistan	3
Burundi	5
Eritrea	6
Ethiopia	7
Rwanda	9

135

The striking point seen on these bar graphs is the dominance of China in different fields of production. China joined the World Trade Organization in 2001, and its exports are experiencing a highly successful period, creating a large trade surplus that provides funds for more investments. Its three major trading partners are the USA, Japan and South Korea. By 2004, China produced almost 180 million tonnes of steel, greater than the combined output of the next two largest producers, Japan and the USA.

Two of the bar graphs – production of cement and of television and radio receivers – show that China makes as much as all the other countries in the top ten combined. It also produces over 1.7 million motor vehicles each year, with this number expected to double over the next few years. However, in terms of the gross domestic product (GDP), the total amount of goods and services produced annually by a country, the USA led in 2002 with US$10,400 billion and China was a distant second with US$5,700 billion. The UK was seventh with US$1,520 billion and Australia was sixteenth with US$528 billion.

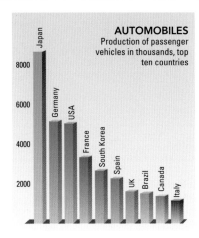

AUTOMOBILES
Production of passenger vehicles in thousands, top ten countries

China is the only major industrial nation listed on the following page among those countries having the largest increase in manufacturing output. Six of the ten nations showing a decrease in manufacturing output were formerly under communist rule.

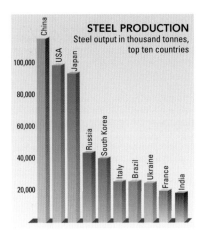

STEEL PRODUCTION
Steel output in thousand tonnes, top ten countries

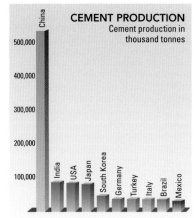

CEMENT PRODUCTION
Cement production in thousand tonnes

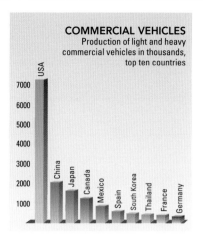

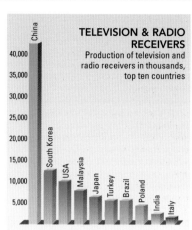

AVERAGE ANNUAL % GROWTH (1990–2001)

LARGEST INCREASE IN MANUFACTURING OUTPUT	
Mozambique	18.0
Uganda	12.8
Laos	12.6
China	12.1
Vietnam	11.2
Syria	10.2
Eritrea	8.8
Malaysia	8.8
Nepal	8.4
Cambodia	8.2

LARGEST DECREASE IN MANUFACTURING OUTPUT	
Haiti	−9.3
Ukraine	−9.0
Burundi	−8.0
Latvia	−6.2
Albania	−5.0
Rwanda	−4.8
Macedonia, (FYROM)	−4.5
Lebanon	−4.3
Moldova	−3.4
Armenia	−3.2

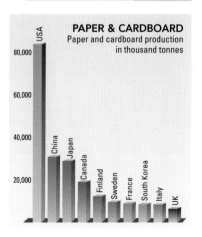

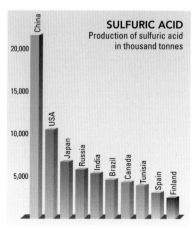

FREIGHT

While ocean passenger traffic is nowadays relatively modest, sea transportation still carries most of the world's trade. Oil and bulk carriers make up the majority of the world fleet, although the general cargo category is the fastest growing. Two innovations have revolutionized sea transportation. The first is the development of the roll-on/roll-off (Ro-Ro) method where lorries or even trains loaded with freight are driven straight on to the ship, thus saving time. The second is containerization in which goods are packed into containers (the dimensions of which are fixed) at the factory, driven to the port and loaded on board by specialist machinery. Almost 30% of world shipping sails under a 'flag of convenience', whereby owners take advantage of low taxs by registering their vessels in a foreign country the ships will never see, notably Panama and Liberia.

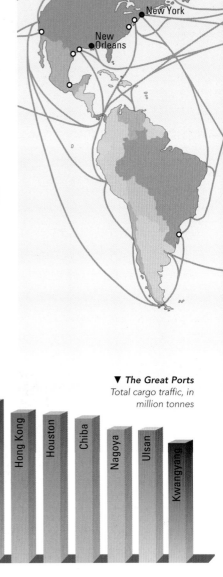

New York

New Orleans

▼ **The Great Ports**
Total cargo traffic, in million tonnes

Singapore · Rotterdam · S. Louisiana · Shanghai · Hong Kong · Houston · Chiba · Nagoya · Ulsan · Kwangyang

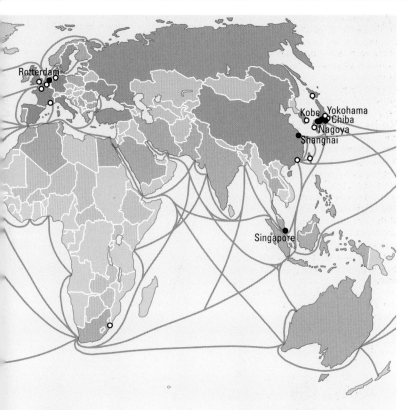

Rotterdam

Kobe
Yokohama
Chiba
Nagoya
Shanghai

Singapore

FREIGHT

Freight unloaded in
millions of tonnes

	Over 100
	50 – 100
	10 – 50
	5 – 10
	Under 5
	Landlocked countries

Major seaports

- Over 100 million tonnes per year

○ 50 – 100 million tonnes per year

—— Major shipping routes

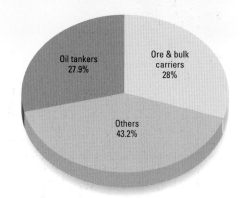

Oil tankers
27.9%

Ore & bulk
carriers
28%

Others
43.2%

▲ *Types of Vessel*
World merchant fleet by type of vessel and deadweight tonnage

139

FINANCE

A country's financial health depends on many volatile factors. Among these are its stock market, international trade balance, the exchange rate of its currency, foreign investment and the nation's budget. The USA is the world's largest borrower, as seen in the pie chart. The recent record deficit of its federal government required its treasury bonds to be purchased by foreign investors. In 2003, foreign investment represented one-third of the US Treasury's debt. The European Union (EU) and USA invest more in each other's economies than they do in any other area. In 2001, the EU represented 49% of investment in the USA and American investment accounted for 46% of the EU total. These figures will increase following the expansion of the EU in 2004.

COUNTRIES THAT EXPORT CAPITAL*

Canada 2.3%
Netherlands 3.3%
China 3.3%
Saudi Arabia 3.6%
Singapore 3.7%
France 3.7%
Hong Kong 3.8%
Taiwan 3.8%
Norway 4.6%
Switzerland 6.2%
Russia 6.2%
Germany 9.8%
Japan 20.8%
Other Countries** 25.2%

COUNTRIES THAT IMPORT CAPITAL*

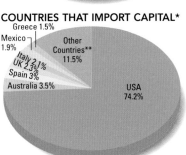

Greece 1.5%
Mexico 1.9%
Italy 2.1%
UK 2.3%
Spain 3%
Australia 3.5%
Other Countries** 11.5%
USA 74.2%

*As measured by countries' current (capital) account surplus (deficit)
**Those countries with shares of total surplus less than 2.3%

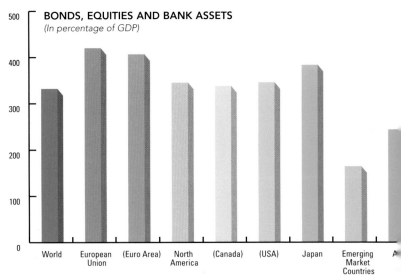

BONDS, EQUITIES AND BANK ASSETS
(In percentage of GDP)

500
400
300
200
100
0

World | European Union | (Euro Area) | North America | (Canada) | (USA) | Japan | Emerging Market Countries

GROSS NATIONAL SAVINGS
as percent of GNI

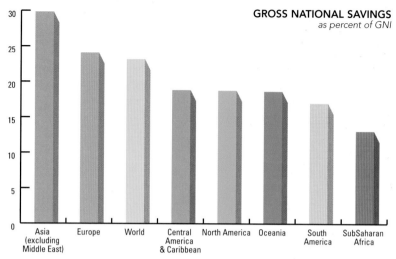

No data for Middle East and North Africa

▲ The bar chart shows the regional gross national savings as a percentage of gross national income. Individuals in Europe save more than the world average and North Americans less. The percentages for individual countries in 2000 include Russia at 35.4%, Canada at 25.3%, Germany at 21.2%, Australia at 18.9%, New Zealand at 18.6%, the USA at 18% and the UK at 15.2%.

◀ A country's capital market is made up of its bonds, equities and bank assets. In 2004, in both the European Union and USA, this amounted to more than US$50,000 billion. Their equity markets together represented 80% of the total global stock market capitalization.

STOCK MARKET CAPITALIZATION
in US$billions

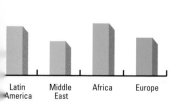

▲ Stock market capitalization is calculated by multiplying the number of outstanding shares by their current market value. An increase means shareholders become richer.

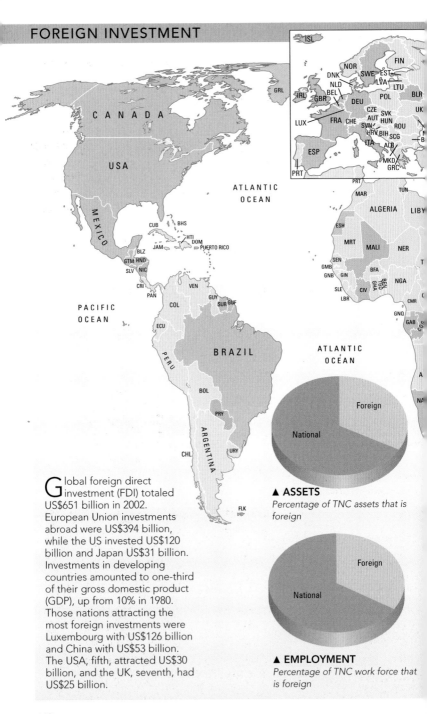

ATLANTIC OCEAN

PACIFIC OCEAN

ATLANTIC OCEAN

CANADA

USA

MEXICO

BRAZIL

ARGENTINA

▲ **ASSETS**
Percentage of TNC assets that is foreign

▲ **EMPLOYMENT**
Percentage of TNC work force that is foreign

Global foreign direct investment (FDI) totaled US$651 billion in 2002. European Union investments abroad were US$394 billion, while the US invested US$120 billion and Japan US$31 billion. Investments in developing countries amounted to one-third of their gross domestic product (GDP), up from 10% in 1980. Those nations attracting the most foreign investments were Luxembourg with US$126 billion and China with US$53 billion. The USA, fifth, attracted US$30 billion, and the UK, seventh, had US$25 billion.

See pages 8 and 9 for country abbreviations

FDI INFLOWS
by host economy in
US$millions

�largeblock	10,000
	1,000 – 9,999
	300 – 999
	100 – 299
	1 – 99
	0/No data

▼ These top transnational corporations (TNCs) are among some 64,000 that control about 870,000 foreign affiliates.

RANKING BY FOREIGN ASSETS		
Corporation	**Home Economy**	**Industry**
Vodafone	UK	Telecommunications
General Electric	USA	Electrical & electronic equipment
BP	UK	Petroleum expl./ref./distr.
Vivendi Universal	France	Diversified
Deutsche Telekom AG	Germany	Telecommunications
Exxonmobil Corporation	USA	Petroleum expl./ref./distr.
Ford Motor Company	USA	Motor vehicles
General Motors	USA	Motor vehicles
Royal Dutch/Shell Group	UK/Netherlands	Petroleum expl./ref./distr.
TotalFinaElf	France	Petroleum expl./ref./distr.

EMPLOYMENT

The map confirms that manufacturing predominates in wealthy countries and agriculture in developing ones. In the last half of the 20th century, a major shift occurred in western nations in the way people made their livelihood, and most jobs are now in the service sector. The USA is a prime example of a country that has changed over the last 150 years from being predominately agricultural to being mainly service based. The service industry accounts for about 75% of US jobs and 70% of the UK's gross domestic product (GDP).

EMPLOYMENT	
(selected countries)	
Singapore	8,860
UK	1,270
Belgium	820
Germany	800
Kuwait	767
Bahrain	660
USA	657
Israel	633

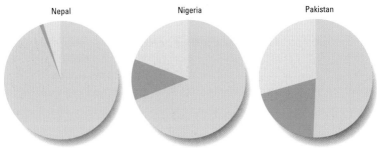

Nepal   Nigeria   Pakistan

Agriculture

Industry

Services

▲ Division of Employment
Distribution of workers between agriculture, industry and services, selected countries
The six countries selected illustrate the typical stages of a country's economic development, the stages range from dependence on agriculture through industrial growth to the expansion of the service sector.

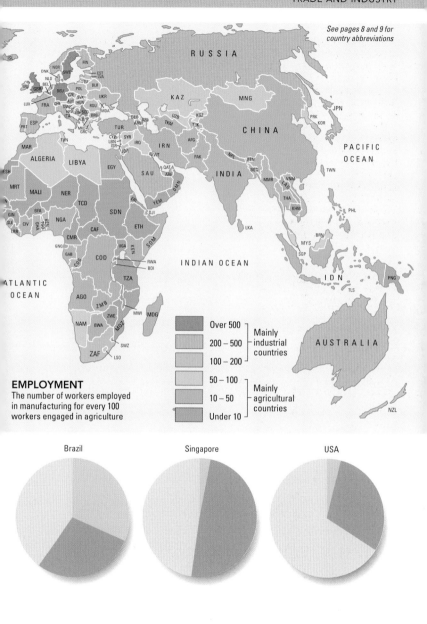

See pages 8 and 9 for country abbreviations

EMPLOYMENT

The number of workers employed in manufacturing for every 100 workers engaged in agriculture

Over 500	Mainly industrial countries
200 – 500	
100 – 200	
50 – 100	Mainly agricultural countries
10 – 50	
Under 10	

Brazil

Singapore

USA

WOMEN'S INCOME

Women have made great strides in most professions but still have fewer executive jobs and lower earnings. In 1991, according to the United Nations' Human Development Report 2003, men in the UK earned an average of US$30,476 and women US$18,180, while the gap in Australia was US$29,945 to US$20,830 and in the USA was US$42,540 to US$26,389 (see **Country Data** p194–203 for full list of global incomes). The bar graphs below show the female economic activity rate (workers and available workers) as a percentage of the men's rate. The rates from 1995 to 2001 were 74% in the UK, 77% in Australia, 80% in New Zealand and 82% in both Canada and the USA.

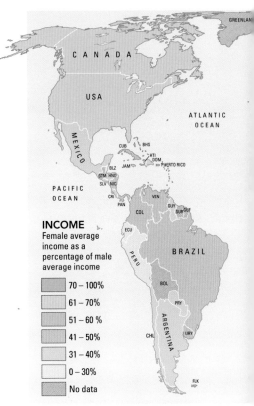

INCOME
Female average income as a percentage of male average income

- 70 – 100%
- 61 – 70%
- 51 – 60 %
- 41 – 50%
- 31 – 40%
- 0 – 30%
- No data

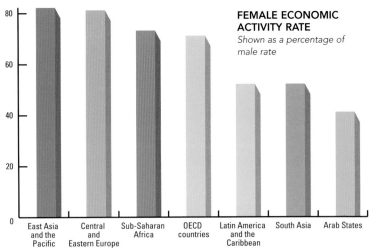

FEMALE ECONOMIC ACTIVITY RATE
Shown as a percentage of male rate

East Asia and the Pacific | Central and Eastern Europe | Sub-Saharan Africa | OECD countries | Latin America and the Caribbean | South Asia | Arab States

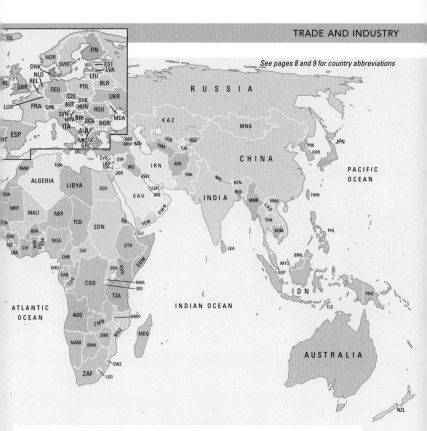

See pages 8 and 9 for country abbreviations

THE PROPORTION OF WOMEN AMONG ADMINISTRATIVE AND MANAGERIAL WORKERS*

	TOP TEN COUNTRIES			BOTTOM TEN COUNTRIES	
1	Poland	66%	1	Qatar	1%
2	Slovakia	60%	2	United Arab Emirates	2%
3	Puerto Rico (US)	59%	3	Iran	2%
4	Sweden	59%	4	Djibouti	2%
5	Hungary	58%	5	Syria	3%
6	New Zealand	55%	6	Solomon Islands	3%
7	Italy	54%	7	Pakistan	4%
8	Portugal	50%	8	Tonga	5%
9	Virgin Islands	49%	9	Kuwait	5%
10	Kazakhstan	48%	10	Bangladesh	5%

*According to the International Standard Classification of Occupations, revised edition (ISCO68), the major group "administrative and managerial workers" includes (a) legislative officials and government administrators and (b) managers. In a few countries the category "administrative and managerial workers" includes the following subgroups: (a) legislators and senior officials; (b) corporate managers; and (c) general managers.

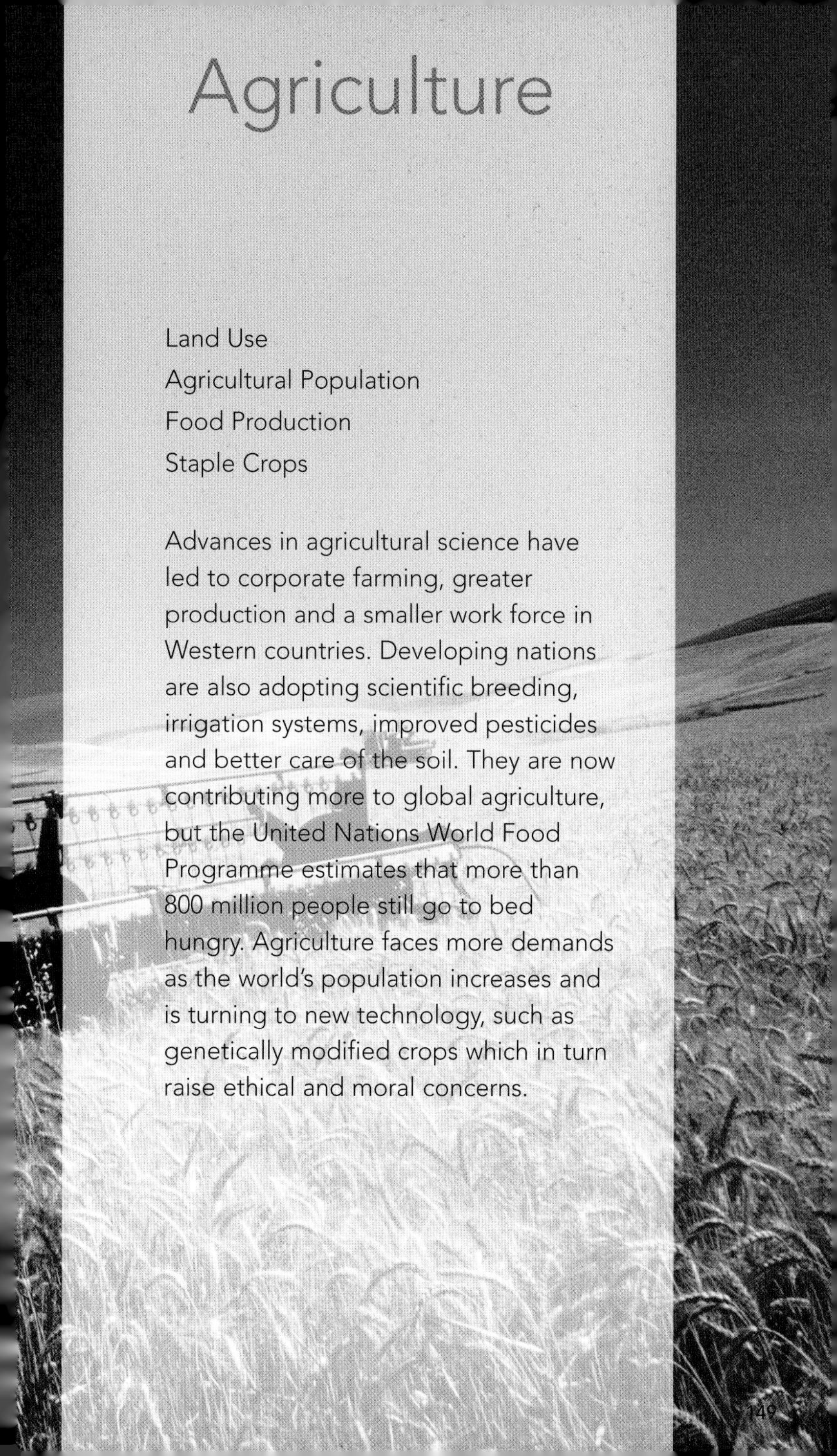

Agriculture

Land Use
Agricultural Population
Food Production
Staple Crops

Advances in agricultural science have led to corporate farming, greater production and a smaller work force in Western countries. Developing nations are also adopting scientific breeding, irrigation systems, improved pesticides and better care of the soil. They are now contributing more to global agriculture, but the United Nations World Food Programme estimates that more than 800 million people still go to bed hungry. Agriculture faces more demands as the world's population increases and is turning to new technology, such as genetically modified crops which in turn raise ethical and moral concerns.

The total arable land in the world is 1.45 billion ha (3.58 billion acres), according to the United Nations Food and Agriculture Organization (FAO). North America has 0.85 ha (2.1 acres) of arable land for each person. The FAO estimates that modern farming methods could grow enough food to feed 33 billion people. (Today's world population is just over 6 billion.) About 4% of the UK's farmland is organically managed on nearly 4,000 organic farms. The move into genetically modified (GM) crops, however, has won little public acceptance in Britain, despite its widespread adoption in other countries, such as the USA. Critics of GM crops question the long-term effects, even though the technique increases yield and resistance to disease.

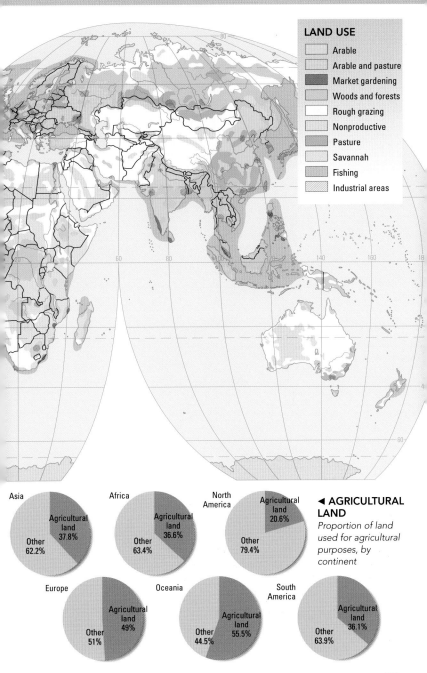

LAND USE

- Arable
- Arable and pasture
- Market gardening
- Woods and forests
- Rough grazing
- Nonproductive
- Pasture
- Savannah
- Fishing
- Industrial areas

Asia
Agricultural land 37.8%
Other 62.2%

Africa
Agricultural land 36.6%
Other 63.4%

North America
Agricultural land 20.6%
Other 79.4%

Europe
Agricultural land 49%
Other 51%

Oceania
Agricultural land 55.5%
Other 44.5%

South America
Agricultural land 36.1%
Other 63.9%

◄ **AGRICULTURAL LAND**
Proportion of land used for agricultural purposes, by continent

The introduction of modern farm machinery and farming methods in the developed world has led to higher yields from a smaller work force. The percentage of the male work force employed in farming from 1995 to 2001 was 6% in Australia, 4% in the USA and 2% in the UK. Yet, three-quarters of the world's work force are still engaged in farming. In India, nearly 600 million people out of 1 billion have their livelihood in agriculture. The developing nations have many crops, such as rice, that are especially labor intensive. The map highlights the north-south (industrial-agricultural) employment divide and the Top 5 table shows that some countries' populations, especially in Africa and Asia, are almost entirely dependent on farm work. The tables also highlight the relative fertility of different countries' land. The climate is too hot and the land too arid in countries like Bahrain to maintain an agricultural population.

See pages 8 and 9 for country abbreviations

RUSSIA

EST
LVA

UKR

MDA

KAZ

MNG

JPN

GEO AZE
ARM

UZB

KGZ

PRK

TUR

TKM

TJK

KOR

CYP SYR
LBN
ISR

IRQ

AFG

CHINA

PACIFIC
OCEAN

JOR

IRN

EGY

KWT

PAK

NPL
BTN

TWN

SAU

QAT
ARE

OMN

INDIA

BGD

MMR

VNM
LAO

ERI

YEM

THA

SDN

DJI

KHM

PHL

ETH

LKA

BRN

UGA

KEN

SOM

MYS

OD

RWA
BDI

SGP

TZA

INDIAN OCEAN

IDN

PNG

MB

MWI

TLS

ZWE

MDG

MOZ

A

SWZ

**AGRICULTURAL
POPULATION**
Percentage of the total population
dependent on agriculture for their
livelihood

AUSTRALIA

LSO

Over 75% dependent

50 – 75% dependent

25 – 50% dependent

10 – 25% dependent

NZL

Under 10% dependent

BOTTOM 5 COUNTRIES		TOP 5 COUNTRIES	
Singapore	0.1%	Bhutan	93.7%
Brunei	0.7%	Nepal	93.0%
Bahrain	1.0%	Burkina Faso	92.3%
Kuwait	1.1%	Burundi	90.4%
Qatar	1.3%	Rwanda	90.3%

FOOD PRODUCTION

Recent history has seen an overproduction of food in the major industrial nations and an undersupply in the Third World. In the 1980s, government farm subsidies helped American and European countries store away 'food mountains'. These have been reduced, but in 1992 it was estimated that Britain alone had enough wheat and barley stored to feed Somalia's population for over a year. The United Nations World Food Programme, set up in 1963, fed 104 million people in 81 countries in 2003. Some developing nations, however, have improved production. Areas of northern Ethiopia, hit by famine in the mid 1980s, are now exporting a food surplus created by improving soil fertility and conserving water.

Situations such as war, sanctions and drought can leave a country in need of food aid. According to the FAO, the top five recipients of cereal food aid in 2002–2003 were Iraq, Ethiopia, the Democratic Republic of Korea, Bangladesh, Afghanistan, and Angola. 60 percent of all cereal aid came from the USA.

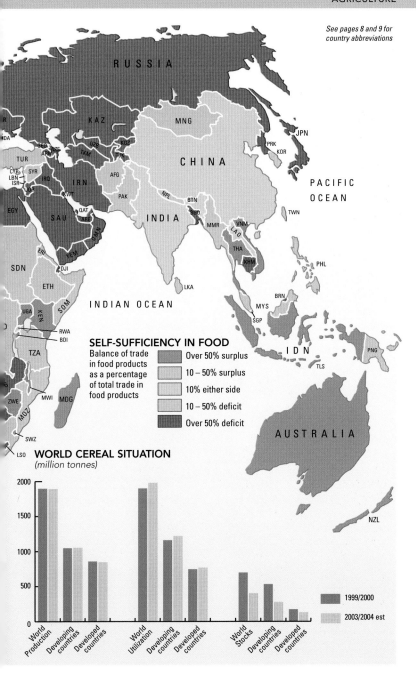

See pages 8 and 9 for country abbreviations

RUSSIA

KAZ

MNG

JPN

PRK
KOR

TUR

CYP SYR
LBN IRQ
ISR
JOR KWT

IRN

AFG

CHINA

PACIFIC
OCEAN

EGY

SAU

QAT
ARE
OMN

PAK

NPL
BTN
BGD

INDIA

MMR

TWN

LAO
VNM

ERI YEM
DJI
SDN
ETH
SOM

THA
KHM

PHL

UGA KEN

RWA
BDI

LKA

INDIAN OCEAN

BRN
MYS

SGP

TZA

IDN

PNG

MWI MDG

ZWE

MOZ

TLS

SWZ

LSO

SELF-SUFFICIENCY IN FOOD
Balance of trade
in food products
as a percentage
of total trade in
food products

Over 50% surplus
10 – 50% surplus
10% either side
10 – 50% deficit
Over 50% deficit

AUSTRALIA

WORLD CEREAL SITUATION
(million tonnes)

NZL

2000

1500

1000

500

0

World
Production

Developing
countries

Developed
countries

World
Utilization

Developing
countries

Developed
countries

World
Stocks

Developing
countries

Developed
countries

1999/2000

2003/2004 est

155

STAPLE CROPS

Key among the staple crops are the cereal grains, such as wheat, oats, rye, millet, corn and rice. These are the world's most important food source.

About 2,000 million tonnes are produced annually, but this must be increased to feed the growing world population. Two other vital food products are

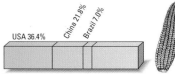

China 18.9% | India 12.2% | USA 11.0% | France 5.7% | Russia 5.6% | Canada 4.6%

World total: 576,317,000 tonnes

Wheat: Grown in a range of climates, with most varieties requiring temperate conditions. Mainly used in baking, it is also used for pasta and breakfast cereals.

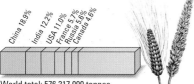

USA 36.4% | China 21.8% | Brazil 7.0%

World total: 590,791,000 tonnes

Corn: An important human food in Africa and Latin America, in the developed world it is processed into breakfast cereals, oil, starches and adhesives. It is also used for animal feed.

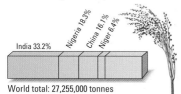

Russia 29.7% | Canada 9.9% | USA 8.2% | Australia 6.7% | Germany 5.6%

World total : 25,953,000 tonnes

Oats: Most widely used to feed livestock, but eaten by humans as oatmeal or porridge. Oats have a beneficial effect on the cardiovascular system, and human consumption is likely to increase.

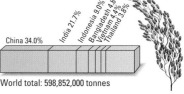

China 34.0% | India 21.7% | Indonesia 9.0% | Bangladesh 4.8% | Vietnam 4.4% | Thailand 3.8%

World total: 598,852,000 tonnes

Rice: The traditional staple food of half the human race. Usually grown standing in water, rice responds well to continuous cultivation, with three or four crops annually.

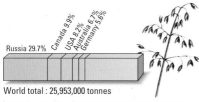

India 33.2% | Nigeria 18.3% | China 16.1% | Niger 6.4%

World total: 27,255,000 tonnes

Millet: The name covers a number of small-grained cereals, members of the grass family. Used to produce flour, meal and animal feed, and fermented to make beer, especially in Africa.

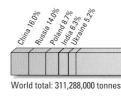

China 16.0% | Russia 14.0% | Poland 8.7% | India 6.3% | Ukraine 5.2%

World total: 311,288,000 tonnes

Potatoes: The most important of the edible tubers, potatoes grow in well-watered, temperate areas. Weight for weight less nutritious than grain, they are a human staple as well as an important animal feed.

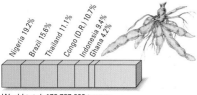

Nigeria 19.2% | Brazil 15.6% | Thailand 11.1% | Congo (D.R.) 10.7% | Indonesia 9.4% | Ghana 4.2%

World total: 172,737,000 tonnes

Cassava: A tropical shrub that needs high rainfall (over 1,000 mm annually) and a 10–30 month growing season to produce its large, edible tubers. Used as flour, as cattle feed and in industrial starches.

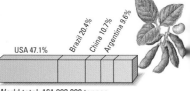

USA 47.1% | Brazil 20.4% | China 10.7% | Argentina 9.6%

World total: 161,993,000 tonnes

Soya: Beans from soya bushes (soybeans) are very high (30–40%) in protein. Most are processed into oil and proprietary protein foods. Consumption since 1950 has tripled, mainly due to the health-conscious developed world.

meat and milk. Global meat production in 2002 totaled 242 million tonnes, with developing nations contributing 56%. Worldwide milk production in 2000 was 579 million tonnes, with the USA and EU accounting for c.35% of this. Australia and New Zealand were major suppliers of processed milk protein products. Developing countries are expected to produce over half of the milk total within a few years.

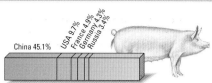

China 45.1% USA 9.7% France 4.9% Germany 4.3% Russia 3.4%

World total: 90,909,000 tonnes

Pork: Although pork is forbidden to many millions, notably Muslims, on religious grounds, more is produced than any other meat in the world, mainly because it is the cheapest. It accounts for about 90% of China's meat output, although per capita meat consumption is relatively low.

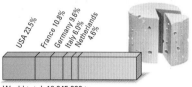

USA 23.5% France 10.8% Germany 9.6% Italy 6.0% Netherlands 4.6%

World total: 16,045,000 tonnes

Cheese: Cheese is milk fermented with selected bacterial strains. The vast majority of cheeses are made from cow's milk, although sheep and goat cheeses are highly prized.

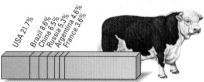

USA 21.7% Brazil 8.6% China 6.5% Russia 5.3% Argentina 4.6% France 3.6%

World total: 57,170,000 tonnes

Beef and Veal: Most beef and veal is reared for home markets, and the top five producers are also the biggest consumers. The USA produces nearly a quarter of the world's beef and eats even more.

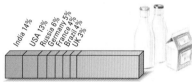

India 14% USA 13% Russia 6% Germany 5% France 4% Brazil 4% UK 3%

World total: 579,085,000 tonnes

Milk: Many human groups, including most Asians, find raw milk indigestible after infancy, and it is often only the starting point for other dairy products such as butter, cheese and yoghurt. Most world production comes from cows, but sheep's milk and goats' milk are also important.

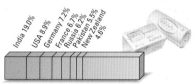

India 19.0% USA 8.9% Germany 7.2% France 6.1% Russia 6.2% Pakistan 5.5% New Zealand 4.6%

World total: 7,049,000 tonnes

Butter: A traditional source of vitamin A as well as calories, butter has lost much popularity in the developed world for health reasons, although it remains a valuable food. Most butter from India, the world's largest producer, is clarified into ghee, which has religious as well as nutritional importance.

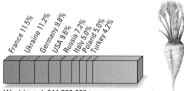

France 11.5% Ukraine 11.2% Germany 9.8% USA 9.6% Russia 7.2% Italy 5.0% Poland 5.0% Turkey 4.2%

World total: 244,780,000 tonnes

Sugar beet: Closely related to the beetroot, sugar beet's yield after processing is indistinguishable from cane sugar. It is replacing sugarcane imports in Europe, to the detriment of the developing countries that rely on it as a major cash crop.

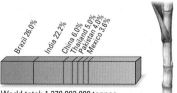

Brazil 26.0% India 22.2% China 6.0% Thailand 5.0% Pakistan 4.0% Mexico 3.6%

World total: 1,278,093,000 tonnes

Sugarcane: Confined to tropical regions, cane sugar accounts for the bulk of international trade in sugar. Most is produced as a foodstuff, but some countries, notably Brazil and South Africa, distill sugarcane to make motor fuels.

Resources

Energy Production
Energy Consumption
Renewable Energy
Mineral Sources
Metals

Natural resources are the life blood of a nation. Their careful management can sustain a country's growth and prosperity. Their reckless exploitation, however, can lead to natural disasters. The present rapid destruction of Brazil's rain forests, for example, diminishes the area's oxygen and contributes to the greenhouse effect and possibly global warming. Energy consumption can also have double-edged consequences. Highly industrialized nations like the USA produce and consume enormous amounts of energy, but this contributes to air pollution. The international ecology movement has condemned fossil fuels and convinced governments to increase their renewable energy sources.

ENERGY PRODUCTION

A country's ability to produce energy is crucial to its economic health. High production leads to national security and wealth, but energy resources can also be exploited or squandered. The map shows Australia and Canada among the world's leading energy producers, and both export most of it. Australia has an abundance of fossil fuel and mineral energy resources. Black coal, Australia's leading energy source for the last 20 years, makes up nearly half of its energy production and uranium is 30% of the total. Canada is the world's largest producer of natural gas and the tenth largest producer of petroleum. These resources make up 77% of Canada's energy production. The bar graphs below show the relatively low reserves held in Western Europe, and the impressive oil and gas reserves of the former Soviet countries.

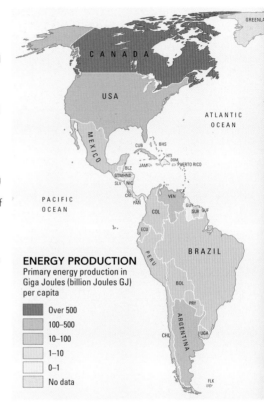

ENERGY PRODUCTION
Primary energy production in Giga Joules (billion Joules GJ) per capita

- Over 500
- 100–500
- 10–100
- 1–10
- 0–1
- No data

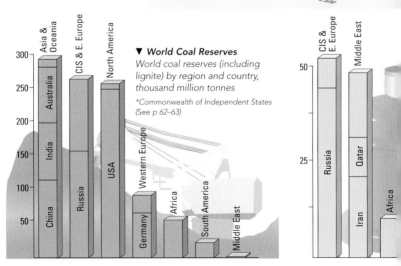

▼ **World Coal Reserves**
World coal reserves (including lignite) by region and country, thousand million tonnes

Commonwealth of Independent States (See p 62–63)

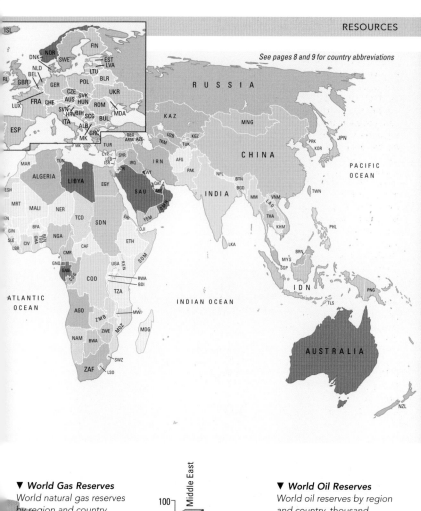

See pages 8 and 9 for country abbreviations

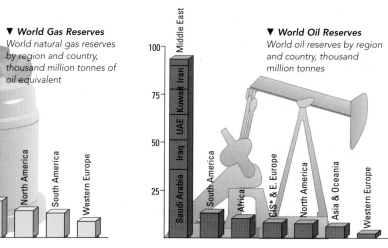

▼ **World Gas Reserves**
World natural gas reserves by region and country, thousand million tonnes of oil equivalent

▼ **World Oil Reserves**
World oil reserves by region and country, thousand million tonnes

161

Although the bar chart shows North America as the leading energy consumer, most of this involves one country, the USA. In 2001, it consumed 97.1 quadrillion Btu compared to Canada's 12.5 quadrillion. The leading European nations were Germany with 14.4, France with 10.5 and the UK with 9.8. Australia consumed 5 and New Zealand 0.8. Third World countries were low consumers, such as Zimbabwe with 0.2 and Brunei with 0.1. Europe and North America were the largest consumers of nuclear energy, while Asia and Oceania depended mostly on coal.

World Energy Consumption
Energy consumed by world regions, measured in million tonnes of oil equivalent. Total world consumption was 9125 MtOe. Only energy from oil, gas, coal, nuclear and hydroelectric sources are included. Excluded are fuels such as wood, peat, animal waste, wind, solar and geothermal which, though important in some countries, are unreliably documented in terms of consumption statistics.

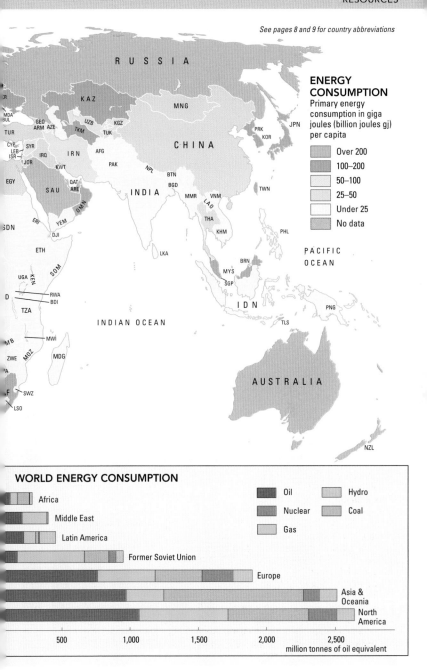

See pages 8 and 9 for country abbreviations

ENERGY CONSUMPTION

Primary energy consumption in giga joules (billion joules gj) per capita

- Over 200
- 100–200
- 50–100
- 25–50
- Under 25
- No data

WORLD ENERGY CONSUMPTION

- Oil
- Nuclear
- Gas
- Hydro
- Coal

Africa
Middle East
Latin America
Former Soviet Union
Europe
Asia & Oceania
North America

500   1,000   1,500   2,000   2,500
million tonnes of oil equivalent

163

RENEWABLE ENERGY

Renewable energy, also called alternative energy, is derived from natural processes which are replenished constantly, like sunlight, wind and water. It is much kinder to the environment than the traditional energy forms of coal, gas and nuclear energy. The UK initiated a Renewable Obligation in 2002 setting a legally binding target to achieve 10.4% of its electricity supply from renewables by 2010. In 2004, this was increased to 15.4% by 2015–16. China, which expects its energy demands to double by 2020, established renewable energy as a basic national policy in 2004. Renewable energy consumption in the USA actually fell from 7 percent of all energy in 1998 to 6 percent in 2002. One reason cited is the higher costs. Two British studies in 2004 found that renewable energy costs

▶ RENEWABLE ENERGY CONSUMPTION

Renewable energy consumption (excl. hydroelectric) Thousand metric tons oil equivalent (ktoe)

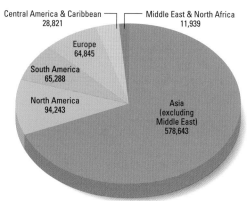

Central America & Caribbean
28,821

Middle East & North Africa
11,939

Europe
64,845

South America
65,288

North America
94,243

Asia
(excluding
Middle East)
578,643

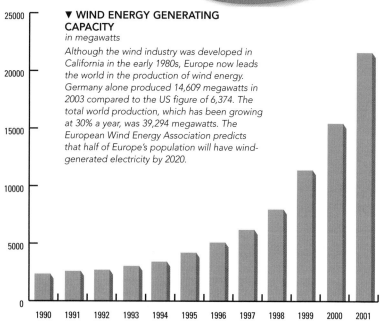

▼ WIND ENERGY GENERATING CAPACITY
in megawatts

Although the wind industry was developed in California in the early 1980s, Europe now leads the world in the production of wind energy. Germany alone produced 14,609 megawatts in 2003 compared to the US figure of 6,374. The total world production, which has been growing at 30% a year, was 39,294 megawatts. The European Wind Energy Association predicts that half of Europe's population will have wind-generated electricity by 2020.

the consumer twice that of fossil fuels or nuclear power. The pie chart on page 164 reveals that Asia uses three times more renewable energy than the rest of the world. This partly reflects the traditional reliance on water and wind power.

Water is one of the oldest sources of power. Today's hydroelectric power plant normally uses a large dam on a river, but hydropower can also be produced by a small canal. Both use the flow to activate a generator to produce electricity. The largest hydroelectric dam is being built in China, the Three Gorges Dam on the Yangtze river. Begun in 1994, it will take 20 years and US$24 billion to complete. The reservoir will stretch 563km (350mi) upstream, and the project has drawn worldwide criticism for its displacement of 1.9 million people.

HYDROELECTRICITY

Major producers by percentage of world total and by percentage of domestic electricity generation

Country	% of world total production	Country	% of hydroelectric as proportion of domestic electricity
1 Canada	13.1%	1 Bhutan	99.9%
2 USA	12.0%	2 Paraguay	99.8%
3 Brazil	11.1%	= Zambia	99.8%
4 China	8.5%	4 Norway	99.1%
5 Russia	6.1%	5 Ethiopia	98.1%
6 Norway	4.6%	6 Congo (Rep. Dem.)	97.9%
7 Japan	3.3%	7 Tajikistan	97.8%
8 India	3.1%	8 Cameroon	97.3%
9 France	2.8%	9 Albania	97.2%
10 Sweden	2.7%	= Laos	97.2%

Countries heavily reliant on hydroelectricity are usually small and nonindustrial: a high proportion of hydroelectric power more often reflects a modest energy budget than vast hydroelectric resources. The USA, for instance, produces only 8.5% of its power requirements from hydroelectricity; yet that 8.5% amounts to more than three times the hydropower generated by most of Africa.

NET GENERATING CAPACITY OF RENEWABLE AND WASTE PRODUCTS (MW)		
	1990	2001
Total Capacity (MW)	393,359	475,113
Hydro	369,129	419,166
Pumped Storage	0	85,801
Wind	2,386	21,630
Geothermal	4,463	5,443
Solar Photovoltaics	0	1,034
Solar Thermal	348	397
Tide/Wave	260	260

◄ *Renewable and Waste Products accounted for 13.8% of the world's total primary energy supply in 2000. Biomass, which is plant material, made up about 80% of the total renewable energy.*

MINERAL SOURCES

Minerals are distributed unevenly and some industrial countries import most of the raw materials they need. Some imports come from mineral-rich countries, such as Australia, but others come from developing nations, especially those in Africa and South America.

Australia's many minerals include coal, bauxite, copper, diamonds, gold, iron ore, nickel, silver, tin, tungsten and zinc. Canada is also rich in mineral resources,

being the world's leading producer of uranium, zinc ore and potash.

Russia, where mining is the most valuable activity, is the world's leading producer of nickel and the second largest manufacturer of aluminum. South Africa produces the most gold and is the fifth largest producer of diamonds. The USA's many minerals include coal, iron ore, gold, diamonds, copper and nickel. Brazil mines iron ore, tin, manganese, aluminum and diamonds.

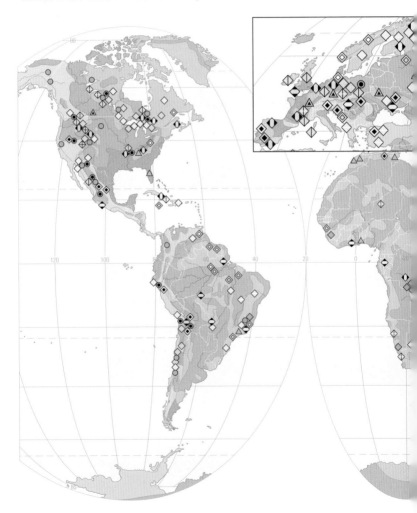

DISTRIBUTION

Iron and ferro-alloys
◇ Chrome
◈ Cobalt
◇ Iron Ore
◈ Manganese
◇ Molybdenum
◇ Nickel Ore
◈ Tungsten

Precious metals and stones
◈ Diamonds
● Gold
◉ Silver

Nonferrous metals
◈ Bauxite (◈ Aluminum)
◇ Copper
◈ Lead
◈ Mercury
◈ Tin
◈ Zinc
◇ Uranium

Fertilizers
△ Phosphates
▲ Potash

STRUCTURAL REGIONS

PreCambrian shields

Sedimentary cover on PreCambrian shields

Paleozoic (Caledonian and Hercynian) folding

Sedimentary cover on Paleozoic folding

Mesozoic folding

Sedimentary cover on Mesozoic folding

Cenozoic (Alpine) folding

Sedimentary cover on Cenozoic folding

Intensive Mesozoic and Cenozoic vulcanism

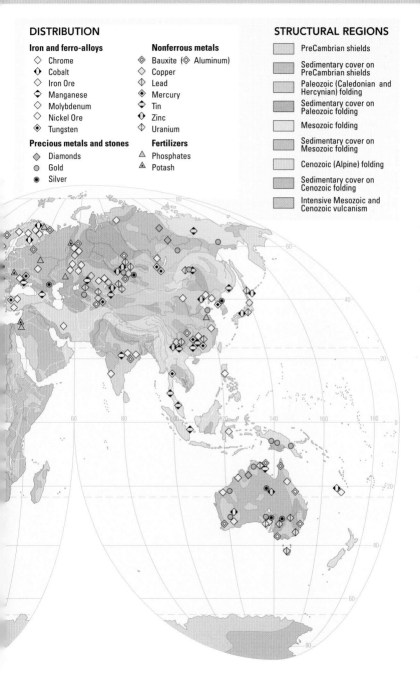

167

METALS

The use of metals played a vital part in the evolving technologies of early peoples. Copper first came into use around 10,000 years ago, bronze about 5,000 years ago, and iron 3,300 years ago. In the early stages of the Industrial Revolution, the location of coal, iron ore and water power usually determined the location of new industries. But due to improvements in transportation, including oil pipelines, industries can now be located almost anywhere.

About three-quarters of the known elements are metals, with aluminum and iron the most abundant. Metals combine to form an alloy, such as brass which has copper and zinc as essential components.

Figures for aluminum are for refined metal; all other figures refer to ore production

STRATEGIC MINERALS

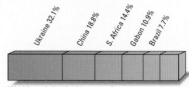

Ukraine 32.1% China 18.8% S. Africa 14.4% Gabon 10.9% Brazil 7.7%

World total: 7,450,000 tonnes (metal content)

▲ **Manganese** *In its pure state, manganese is a hard, brittle metal. Alloyed with chrome, iron and nickel, it produces abrasion-resistant steels; manganese-aluminum alloys are light but tough. Found in batteries and inks, manganese is also used in glass production.*

ALUMINUM

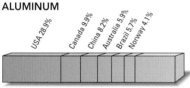

USA 28.9% Canada 9.9% China 8.2% Australia 5.9% Brazil 5.7% Norway 4.1%

World total: 23,900,000 tonnes*

▲ **Aluminum** *Lightweight and corrosion resistant, aluminum alloys are widely used in aircraft, vehicles, cans and packaging.*

COPPER

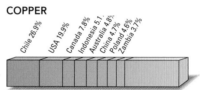

Chile 26.9% USA 19.9% Canada 7.8% Indonesia 5.1% Australia 4.8% China 4.7% Poland 4.6% Zambia 3.7%

World total: 12,900,000 tonnes*

▲ **Copper** *An excellent conductor of heat and electricity, it forms part of most electrical items.*

TIN

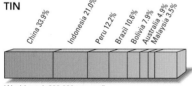

China 33.9% Indonesia 21.0% Peru 12.2% Brazil 10.6% Bolivia 7.9% Australia 4.9% Malaysia 3.5%

World total: 200,000 tonnes*

◄ **Tin** *Soft, pliable and nontoxic, used to coat 'tin' (tin-plated steel) cans, in the manufacture of foils and in alloys. The principal tin-bearing mineral is cassiterite (SnO2), found in ore formed from molten rock.*

ZINC

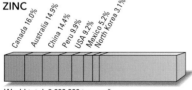

Canada 16.0% Australia 14.9% China 14.4% Peru 9.9% USA 9.2% Mexico 5.2% North Korea 3.1%

World total: 8,000,000 tonnes*

◄ **Zinc** *Often found in association with lead ores, zinc is highly resistant to corrosion, and about 40% of the refined metal is used to plate sheet steel, particularly vehicle bodies – a process known as galvanizing. Zinc is also used in dry batteries, paints and dyes.*

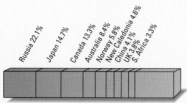

World total: 1,230,000 tonnes

▲ **Nickel** Combined with chrome and iron, nickel produces stainless and high-strength steels; similar alloys go to make magnets and electrical heating elements. Nickel combined with copper is widely used to make coins; cupro-nickel alloy is very resistant to corrosion.

World total: 13,700,000 tonnes

▲ **Chromium** Most of the world's chromium production is alloyed with iron and other metals to produce steels with various different properties. Chromium is also used in the production of refractory bricks, and its salts for tanning and dyeing leather and cloth.

LEAD

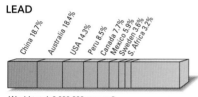

World total: 2,980,000 tonnes *

▲ **Lead** Its use in vehicle batteries accounts for the USA's prime consumer status; lead is also made into sheeting and piping.

MERCURY

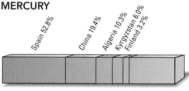

World total: 1,800 tonnes *

▲ **Mercury** Most mercury production is used in antifungal and antifouling preparations, and to make detonators.

▶ **Gold** Regarded for centuries as the most valuable metal in the world and used to make coins, gold is still recognized as the monetary standard. A soft metal, it is alloyed to make jewelry; the electronics industry values its corrosion resistance and conductivity.

GOLD

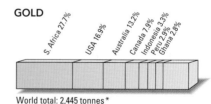

World total: 2,445 tonnes *

SILVER

World total: 17,900 tonnes *

◀ **Silver** Most silver comes from ores mined and processed for other metals (including lead and copper). Pure or alloyed with harder metals, it is used for jewelry and ornaments. Industrial use includes dentistry, electronics, photography and as a chemical catalyst.

Communications and Leisure

Telephones

Computers and the Internet

Radio and Television

Books and Newspapers

Music

Cinema

Sport – The Olympic Games

Sport – Soccer

Travel and Tourism

All forms of communication can be used for work, pleasure and information. This is true for individual telephone calls, e-mails and letters, as well as mass communication forms, such as the Internet, television, radio, newspapers, magazines and books. Some popular leisure activities like listening to music or watching films, plays and sport, are mostly for pure enjoyment but can also provide revealing information about a culture. The constantly expanding field of international travel and tourism offers the additional face-to-face experience of learning about other cultures.

TELEPHONES

The map to the right shows the number of telephone landlines per 100 people, while the map below shows the number of cell phones per 100 people. The maps show that despite recent advances in telecommunications, including the growth of the Internet and the development of powerful fourth generation cell phones, there remains a large discrepancy between the wealthier nations and those considered 'developing'.

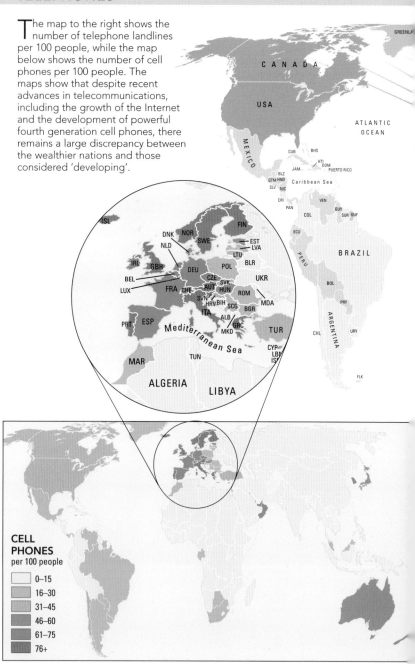

CELL PHONES
per 100 people

- 0–15
- 16–30
- 31–45
- 46–60
- 61–75
- 76+

See pages 8 and 9 for country abbreviations

LANDLINES
per 100 people

- 76+
- 61–75
- 46–60
- 31–45
- 16–30
- 0–15
- No data

25 countries with highest cell phone usage per 100 people

Luxembourg	96.7
Italy	83.9
Norway	82.5
Iceland	82.0
Israel	80.8
Austria	80.7
Sweden	79.0
United Kingdom	78.3
Finland	77.8
Portugal	77.4
Slovenia	76.0
Greece	75.1
Belgium	74.7
Netherlands	73.9
Denmark	73.7
Ireland	72.9
Singapore	72.4
Switzerland	72.4
United Arab Emirates	72.0
Germany	68.3
Czech Republic	65.9
Spain	65.5
Oman	62.8
New Zealand	62.1
South Korea	60.8

TOP 20 TELECOMMUNICATION OPERATORS

ranked by revenue

Operator	Country	Revenue total (US$ million)
NTT	Japan	97,953
AT&T	USA	62,391
SBC	USA	49,489
MCI Worldcom	USA	37,120
Deutsche Telekom	Germany	35,750
BT	UK	34,955
Bell Atlantic	USA	33,174
China Telecom	China	27,539
France Télécom	France	27,344
Telecom Italia	Italy	27,229
GTE	USA	25,336
BellSouth	USA	25,224
Telefónica	Spain	23,051
Sprint	USA	19,928
DDI	Japan	14,396
Vodafone	UK	14,183
US West	USA	13,182
Telstra	Australia	12,046
Telmex	Mexico	10,132
KPN	Netherlands	9,169

COMPUTERS AND THE INTERNET

USA
62.5
PC users
per 100 people

Denmark
57.7
PC users per
100 people

Costa Rica
17.0
PC users per
100 people

CANADA

USA

MEXICO

CUB   BHS
HTI
DOM
JAM   PUERTO RICO
BLZ
GTM HND
SLV NIC
CRI
PAN
COL
ECU
VEN
GUY GUF
SUR

ATLANTIC
OCEAN

PACIFIC
OCEAN

PERU

BRAZIL

ATLANTIC
OCEAN

BOL

PRY

ARGENTINA

CHL   URY

FLK

ISL
NOR   FIN
DNK   SWE EST
NLD   LVA LTU
GBR BEL   POL   BLR
IRL   DEU
CZE SVK
FRA CHE AUT HUN   UKF
LUX   SVN ROU
HRV BIH SCG
ITA   ALB
ESP   MKD
GRC
PRT

PRT
MAR   TUN
ALGERIA   LIB
ESH
MRT
MALI   NER
SEN
GMB   BFA
GNB GIN
SLE CIV   NGA
LBR
CMR
GNQ
GAB

The personal computer, or PC, eased the process of writing and compiling information, and the Internet revolutionized communications and research. The first widely marketed PCs appeared in the 1970s and the Internet's World Wide Web became easily accessible by the 1990s. The map shows the number of PC users per 100 people by nations in 2002. The bar graph adds Internet users, with the USA the only country compared to world regions. The top countries by Internet usage per 100 people in 2002 were Iceland with 64.9%, Sweden with 57.3%, South Korea with 55.2%, the USA with 55.1% and Japan with 54.5%. The top nations using the newer high-speed broadband access to the Internet are South Korea with 21.9 subscribers out of every 100 people, Canada with 11.1, Taiwan with 9.4 and Belgium with 8.4. Broadband usage is expected to increase over the next few years.

The actual number of Internet users is much higher than indicated here as many people share Internet hosts stationed in cafés, libraries and schools.

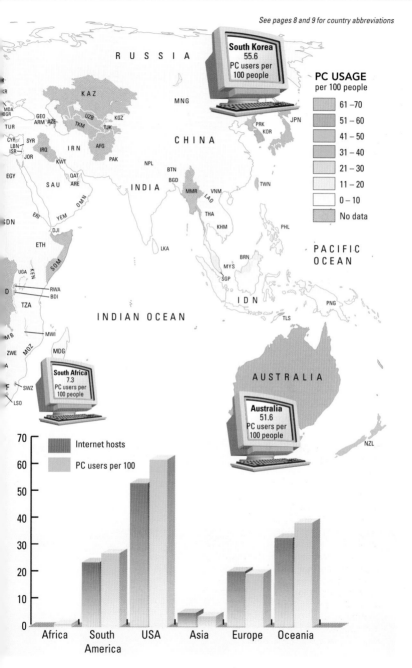

See pages 8 and 9 for country abbreviations

PC USAGE
per 100 people

	61 – 70
	51 – 60
	41 – 50
	31 – 40
	21 – 30
	11 – 20
	0 – 10
	No data

South Korea
55.6
PC users per
100 people

South Africa
7.3
PC users per
100 people

Australia
51.6
PC users per
100 people

RUSSIA

KAZ

MNG

CHINA

JPN

PRK
KOR

INDIA

PACIFIC
OCEAN

INDIAN OCEAN

IDN

AUSTRALIA

NZL

Internet hosts
PC users per 100

Africa | South America | USA | Asia | Europe | Oceania

175

RADIO AND TELEVISION

The map shows the number of televisions per 1,000 people. The proportion of television sets per population is directly linked with the wealth of a nation. In the USA, television ownership has reached saturation point, with an average of 2.4 sets per household. Televisions are no longer considered luxury items and more than half the households in the lowest income bracket have cable or satellite television, a stereo, or a video recorder. The popularity of cable and satellite television has opened up the world market. CNN International can be seen in 212 countries and territories, making it the world's largest TV network. The graphic below shows the number of radios per 1,000 people. Radio continues to be popular and there are currently about 12,850 stations in the US alone. Digital radio is aiding a resurgence in interest, while the invention of the wind-up radio has made the medium accessible to some of the world's most remote areas.

TELEVISIONS
per 1,000 people

- 601–800
- 451–600
- 251–450
- 101–250
- 26–100
- 0–25
- No data available

					Highest number of radios per 1,000 people				
Netherlands Antilles	Canada	Samoa	Iceland	Estonia	Denmark	UK	Finland	Australia	US
1,036.1	1,047.1	1,065.5	1,081.1	1,095.7	1,349.3	1,432.0	1,622.6	1,908.0	2,117.5
22.3	35.3	39.2	43.5	43.9	49.4	50.2	52.4	53.5	55.4
Azerbaijan	Burkina Faso	Nepal	Guinea-Bissau	Mozambique	B'ladesh	Bhutan	Guinea	Lesotho	Haiti
					Lowest number of radios per 1,000 people				

In 1895 Guglielmo Marconi sent the first radio signal. Today, it is estimated that there are more than 600 million radios in use in the United States. The average American household has 5.6 radio receivers. Americans over the age of 12 listen to the radio for an average of 3.2 hours daily. California has just under 900 radio stations, the most stations per state in the US.

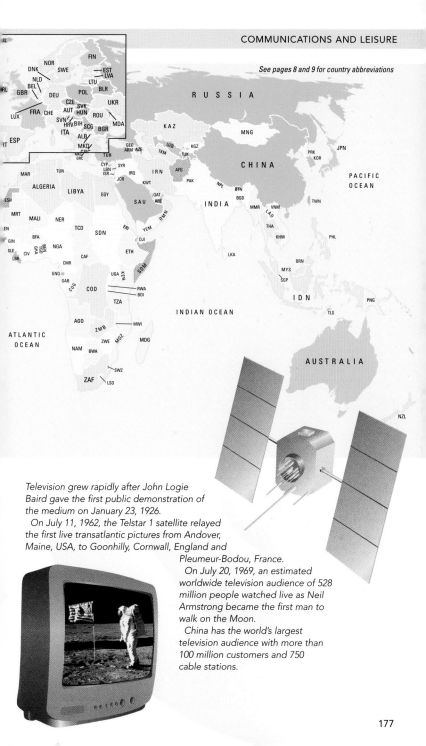

See pages 8 and 9 for country abbreviations

Television grew rapidly after John Logie Baird gave the first public demonstration of the medium on January 23, 1926.

On July 11, 1962, the Telstar 1 satellite relayed the first live transatlantic pictures from Andover, Maine, USA, to Goonhilly, Cornwall, England and Pleumeur-Bodou, France.

On July 20, 1969, an estimated worldwide television audience of 528 million people watched live as Neil Armstrong became the first man to walk on the Moon.

China has the world's largest television audience with more than 100 million customers and 750 cable stations.

177

BOOKS AND NEWSPAPERS

The map of books produced from 1995–1999 does not take populations into account. The US population is five times that of the UK, but both have produced more than 30,000 books a year. Production costs also vary from country to country and may explain why some countries produce so few books. The top seven popular authors on the next page are writers of mysteries, political tracts, science fiction, romance, children's books, dramas and fairy tales.

NEWSPAPER CIRCULATION

HIGHEST CIRCULATION

The top circulating US newspaper at the beginning of 2004 was USA Today with 2,251,035 readers worldwide.

Newspaper circulation bar chart:
- Japan: 72,705
- US: 56,990
- China: 48,600
- Germany: 25,500
- UK: 19,332
- Rep. of Korea: 17,700
- Russian Fed.: 15,517
- France: 12,700
- Mexico: 9,030
- Turkey: 6,845

NUMBER OF BOOKS
Average number produced per year

- 30,000+
- 10,001 – 30,000
- 5,001 – 10,000
- 1,001 – 5,000
- 1 – 1,000
- No data

LOWEST CIRCULATION

The appearance of so many Third World countries on this pie chart is partly a reflection of illiteracy rates.

Lowest circulation pie chart:
- Seychelles
- San Marino
- Niger
- Gambia
- French Guiana
- Equatorial Guinea
- Cook Islands
- Chad
- Rwanda
- Greenland

See pages 8 and 9 for country abbreviations

THE TOP FIFTEEN MOST TRANSLATED AUTHORS

	Author	Number of translations
1	Agatha Christie	5,268
2	Vladimir Ilyich Lenin	3,457
3	Jules Verne	3,367
4	Barbara Cartland	2,967
5	Enid Blyton	2,958
6	William Shakespeare	2,617
7	Hans Christian Andersen	2,116
8	Jakob Grimm	2,011
9	Wilhelm Grimm	2,006
10	Stephen King	1,933
11	Danielle Steel	1,906
12	Alexandre Dumas	1,841
13	Isaac Asimov	1,769
14	Mark Twain	1,679
15	Jack London	1,618

BOOKS TRANSLATED INTO TARGET LANGUAGE

	Target language	Titles translated
1	German	217,483
2	Spanish	163,036
3	French	133,449
4	English	91,496
5	Japanese	78,162
6	Dutch	63,712
7	Russian	59,578
8	Portuguese	44,744
9	Polish	38,654
10	Danish	38,135

North America
41%
$13.2 bn

Europe
34%
$11.1 bn

Latin America
3%
$1 bn

Middle East and Africa
1%
$0.3 bn

Music is a universal language, but this map shows that the USA and Europe buy 75% of the commercial product. The top US genre in 2003 was rock, named by 25% of those polled as their favorite. Others named were rap/hip-hop by 13.5%, r&b/urban music by 11.2%, and country and pop, both by 9%. Some countries are concerned about the popularity of US-based acts compared to native acts. In France, radio broadcasters are required by law to play at least 40% music sung in French.

CDs sold US$2 billion worldwide in 2003, and the relatively new format of DVD music videos made US$1.8 billion. Internet downloads are quickly increasing: Apple's iTunes hit the 50 million-download mark in March 2004. Music bosses link this trend with falling music sales globally.

Concert tours remain popular and can generate huge profits; in 2002 in North America, the Rolling Stones tour of 33 cities grossed US$87.9 million and the Billy Joel and Elton John tour of 14 cities made US$65.5 million.

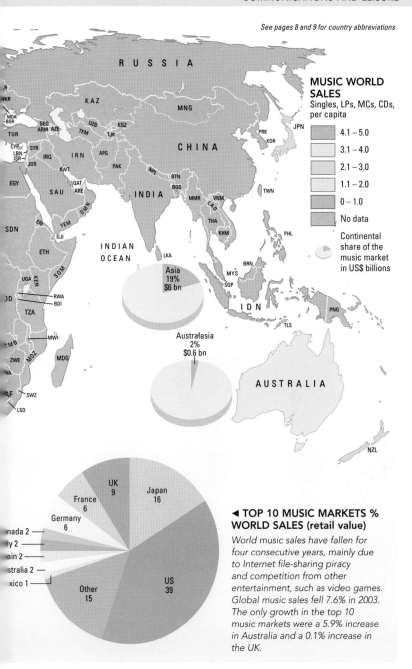

See pages 8 and 9 for country abbreviations

MUSIC WORLD SALES
Singles, LPs, MCs, CDs, per capita

- 4.1 – 5.0
- 3.1 – 4.0
- 2.1 – 3.0
- 1.1 – 2.0
- 0 – 1.0
- No data

Continental share of the music market in US$ billions

Asia
19%
$6 bn

Australasia
2%
$0.6 bn

Top 10 Music Markets % (pie chart):
- Japan 16
- UK 9
- France 6
- Germany 6
- Canada 2
- Italy 2
- Spain 2
- Australia 2
- Mexico 1
- Other 15
- US 39

◄ TOP 10 MUSIC MARKETS % WORLD SALES (retail value)

World music sales have fallen for four consecutive years, mainly due to Internet file-sharing piracy and competition from other entertainment, such as video games. Global music sales fell 7.6% in 2003. The only growth in the top 10 music markets were a 5.9% increase in Australia and a 0.1% increase in the UK.

CINEMA

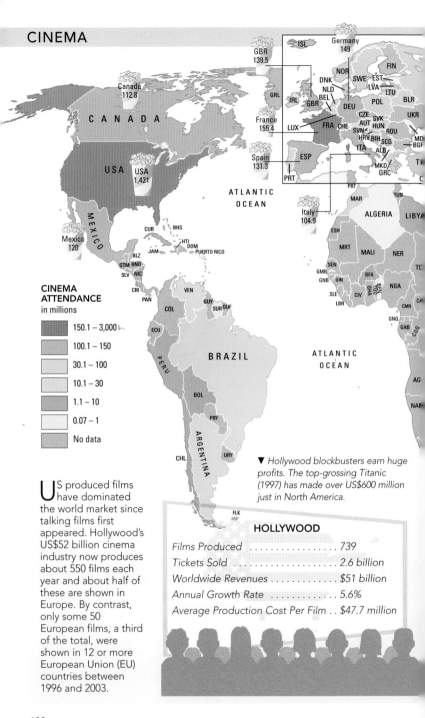

Cinema Attendance (in millions):
- GBR 139.5
- Germany 149
- France 155.4
- Spain 131.3
- Canada 112.8
- USA 1,421
- Italy 104.9
- Mexico 120

CINEMA ATTENDANCE
in millions

	150.1 – 3,000
	100.1 – 150
	30.1 – 100
	10.1 – 30
	1.1 – 10
	0.07 – 1
	No data

U S produced films have dominated the world market since talking films first appeared. Hollywood's US$52 billion cinema industry now produces about 550 films each year and about half of these are shown in Europe. By contrast, only some 50 European films, a third of the total, were shown in 12 or more European Union (EU) countries between 1996 and 2003.

▼ Hollywood blockbusters earn huge profits. The top-grossing Titanic (1997) has made over US$600 million just in North America.

HOLLYWOOD

Films Produced	739
Tickets Sold	2.6 billion
Worldwide Revenues	$51 billion
Annual Growth Rate	5.6%
Average Production Cost Per Film	$47.7 million

See pages 8 and 9 for country abbreviations

India
2,860

Indonesia
190

▼ India's film industry grew by 15%
annually from 1997 to 2002, with
increasing popularity among Western
audiences.

BOLLYWOOD

Films Produced 1,013
Tickets Sold . . . . 3.6 billion
Worldwide Revenues . . . . $1.3 billion
Annual Growth Rate 12.6%
Average Production Cost Per Film . . $1.5 million

European production is
small next to India's
annual cinema output.
France is the leader
making an average of 200
films a year. Britain spent
about US$24 million on 20
films between 2000 and
2003, and they made
US$230 at the box office.
The UK Film Council
spends some US$110
million annually on all
types of films.

The modern Olympics, based on the ancient Greek games, began in 1896 to build better international understanding through sport. Although a 'winning' nation is supposedly not recorded, medal counts have been used to boost national pride and even political systems. The map reflects the large numbers won by the USA and USSR during the Cold War. The winter games began in 1924, and there are also now Paralympics for the disabled and Special Olympics 'empowering individuals with mental retardation'. The 2008 summer Olympics will be in Beijing, China, while future winter Olympic venues are Turin, Italy in 2006 and Vancouver, Canada in 2010.

ATHENS THEN AND NOW

1896 Olympics Athens		2004 Olympics Athens	
Countries	14	Countries	201
Athletes	241	Athletes	10,500
Sports	9	Sports	28

See pages 8 and 9 for country abbreviations

OLYMPIC GAMES
Medals won in Summer Olympics (1896 – 2000)

- 701+
- 301 – 700
- 101 – 300
- 21 – 100
- 1 – 20
- No medals

Includes medals won when part of former USSR

Includes medals won when divided as West and East Germany

Includes medals won when part of Czechoslovakia

Summer Olympic venues

1 Athens, Greece 1896, 2004
2 Paris, France 1900, 1924
3 St. Louis, USA 1904
4 London, UK 1908, 1948
5 Stockholm, Sweden 1912
6 Antwerp, Belgium 1920
7 Amsterdam, Netherlands 1928
8 Los Angeles, USA 1932, 1984
9 Berlin, Germany 1936
10 Helsinki, Finland 1952
11 Melbourne, Australia 1956
12 Rome, Italy 1960
13 Tokyo, Japan 1964
14 Mexico City, Mexico 1968
15 Munich, Germany 1972
16 Montreal, Canada 1976
17 Moscow, USSR 1980
18 Seoul, South Korea 1988
19 Barcelona, Spain 1992
20 Atlanta, USA 1996
21 Sydney, Australia 2000

Winter Olympic venues

22 Chamonix, France 1924
   Grenoble, France 1968
   Albertville, France 1992
23 St. Moritz, Switzerland 1928, 1948
24 Lake Placid, USA 1932, 1980
25 Garmisch-Partenkirchen, Germany 1936
26 Oslo, Norway 1952
   Lillehammer, Norway 1994
27 Cortina d'Ampezzo, Italy 1956
28 Squaw Valley, USA 1960
29 Innsbruck, Austria 1964, 1976
30 Sapporo, Japan 1972
   Nagano, Japan 1998
31 Sarajevo, Yugoslavia 1984
32 Calgary, Canada 1988
33 Salt Lake City, USA 2002

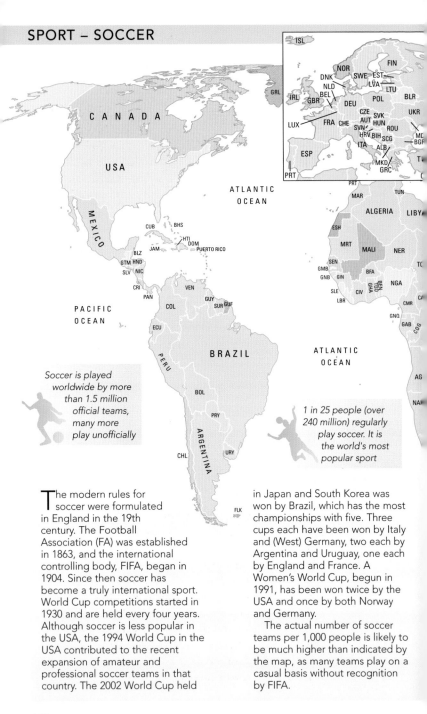

Soccer is played worldwide by more than 1.5 million official teams, many more play unofficially

1 in 25 people (over 240 million) regularly play soccer. It is the world's most popular sport

The modern rules for soccer were formulated in England in the 19th century. The Football Association (FA) was established in 1863, and the international controlling body, FIFA, began in 1904. Since then soccer has become a truly international sport. World Cup competitions started in 1930 and are held every four years. Although soccer is less popular in the USA, the 1994 World Cup in the USA contributed to the recent expansion of amateur and professional soccer teams in that country. The 2002 World Cup held in Japan and South Korea was won by Brazil, which has the most championships with five. Three cups each have been won by Italy and (West) Germany, two each by Argentina and Uruguay, one each by England and France. A Women's World Cup, begun in 1991, has been won twice by the USA and once by both Norway and Germany.

The actual number of soccer teams per 1,000 people is likely to be much higher than indicated by the map, as many teams play on a casual basis without recognition by FIFA.

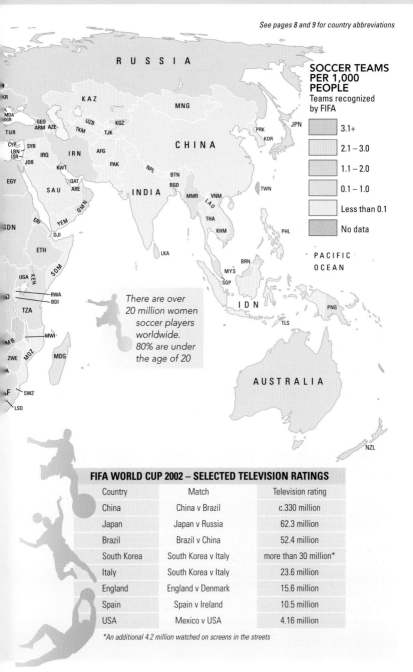

See pages 8 and 9 for country abbreviations

SOCCER TEAMS PER 1,000 PEOPLE

Teams recognized by FIFA

	3.1+
	2.1 – 3.0
	1.1 – 2.0
	0.1 – 1.0
	Less than 0.1
	No data

There are over 20 million women soccer players worldwide. 80% are under the age of 20

FIFA WORLD CUP 2002 – SELECTED TELEVISION RATINGS

Country	Match	Television rating
China	China v Brazil	c.330 million
Japan	Japan v Russia	62.3 million
Brazil	Brazil v China	52.4 million
South Korea	South Korea v Italy	more than 30 million*
Italy	South Korea v Italy	23.6 million
England	England v Denmark	15.6 million
Spain	Spain v Ireland	10.5 million
USA	Mexico v USA	4.16 million

*An additional 4.2 million watched on screens in the streets

187

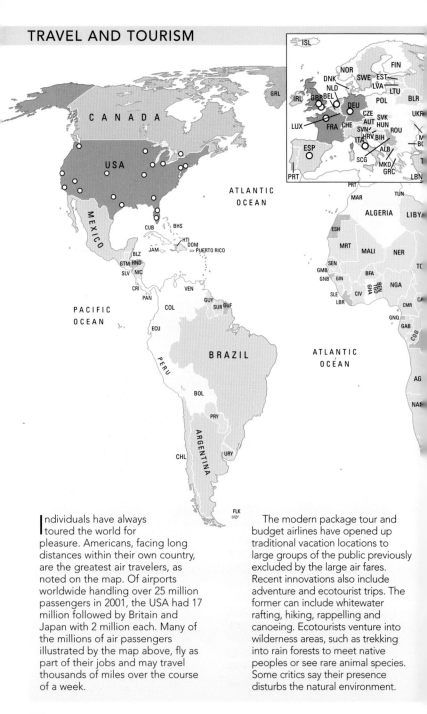

Individuals have always toured the world for pleasure. Americans, facing long distances within their own country, are the greatest air travelers, as noted on the map. Of airports worldwide handling over 25 million passengers in 2001, the USA had 17 million followed by Britain and Japan with 2 million each. Many of the millions of air passengers illustrated by the map above, fly as part of their jobs and may travel thousands of miles over the course of a week.

The modern package tour and budget airlines have opened up traditional vacation locations to large groups of the public previously excluded by the large air fares. Recent innovations also include adventure and ecotourist trips. The former can include whitewater rafting, hiking, rappelling and canoeing. Ecotourists venture into wilderness areas, such as trekking into rain forests to meet native peoples or see rare animal species. Some critics say their presence disturbs the natural environment.

See pages 8 and 9 for country abbreviations

BUSIEST PASSENGER AIRPORTS

Airport	Total Passengers
Atlanta, USA (ATL)	76,876,000
Chicago, USA (ORD)	66,566,000
London/Heathrow, UK (LHR)	63,339,000
Tokyo, Japan (HND)	61,079,000
Los Angeles, USA (LAX)	56,224,000
Dallas/Fort Worth Airport, USA (DFW)	52,829,000
Frankfurt/Main, Germany (FRA)	48,450,000
Paris/Charles De Gaulle, France (CDG)	48,350,000
Amsterdam, Netherlands (AMS)	40,736,000
Denver, USA (DEN)	35,651,000

AIR TRAVEL

Passenger km flown (the number of passengers multiplied by the distance flown from the airport of origin)

- Over 100,000 million
- 50,000 – 100,000 million
- 10,000 – 50,000 million
- 1,000 – 10,000 million
- Under 1,000 million
- No data

○ Airports handling over 25 million passengers

TRAVEL AND TOURISM

Many factors influence a tourist's choice of destinations. The area may have famous attractions, such as Florida's beaches and theme parks, or offer preferable seasonal weather. Price is a large consideration, with the weak dollar in 2004 luring many Europeans to the USA. War and terrorism can deter the tourist trade, as happened in Bali following the bombing there in October 2002. Even the cinema has an impact, with tourism to New Zealand soaring after the Lord of the Rings trilogy was filmed there. New countries can become popular destinations through advertising or, in the case of China, by easing travel restrictions. Libya's 2004 successful negotiations with the Western countries is expected to open its impressive Roman ruins to waves of Western tourists.

▼ *The pie charts indicate the large numbers of tourists worldwide. The 700 million mark was surpassed for the first time in 2002, according to the World Tourism Organization. The large pie chart shows Europe receiving over half of the total number of tourists. Two-thirds of the UK's visitors come from Europe.*

Europe 399.8 million

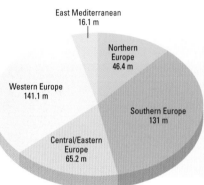

East Mediterranean 16.1 m
Northern Europe 46.4 m
Western Europe 141.1 m
Southern Europe 131 m
Central/Eastern Europe 65.2 m

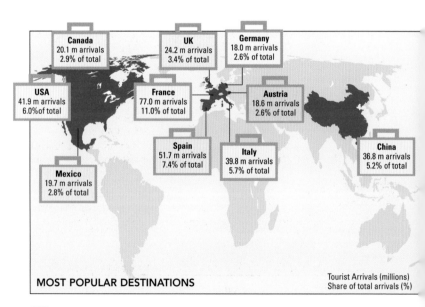

Canada 20.1 m arrivals 2.9% of total

UK 24.2 m arrivals 3.4% of total

Germany 18.0 m arrivals 2.6% of total

USA 41.9 m arrivals 6.0% of total

France 77.0 m arrivals 11.0% of total

Austria 18.6 m arrivals 2.6% of total

Mexico 19.7 m arrivals 2.8% of total

Spain 51.7 m arrivals 7.4% of total

Italy 39.8 m arrivals 5.7% of total

China 36.8 m arrivals 5.2% of total

MOST POPULAR DESTINATIONS

Tourist Arrivals (millions)
Share of total arrivals (%)

INTERNATIONAL TOURIST ARRIVALS PER REGION

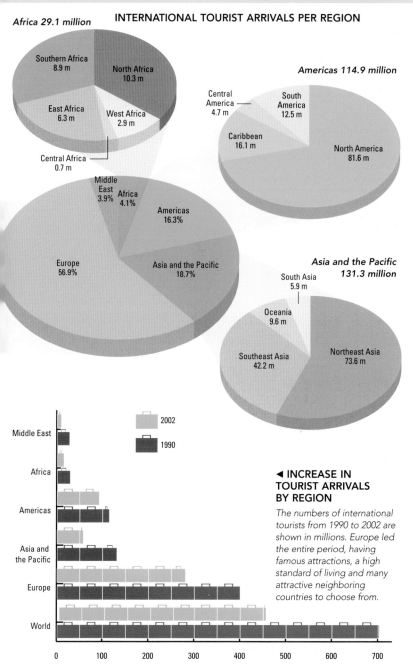

Africa 29.1 million

Southern Africa
8.9 m

North Africa
10.3 m

East Africa
6.3 m

West Africa
2.9 m

Central Africa
0.7 m

Americas 114.9 million

Central America
4.7 m

South America
12.5 m

Caribbean
16.1 m

North America
81.6 m

Middle East
3.9%

Africa
4.1%

Americas
16.3%

Europe
56.9%

Asia and the Pacific
18.7%

*Asia and the Pacific
131.3 million*

South Asia
5.9 m

Oceania
9.6 m

Southeast Asia
42.2 m

Northeast Asia
73.6 m

2002

1990

Middle East

Africa

Americas

Asia and
the Pacific

Europe

World

0   100   200   300   400   500   600   700

◄ INCREASE IN TOURIST ARRIVALS BY REGION

The numbers of international tourists from 1990 to 2002 are shown in millions. Europe led the entire period, having famous attractions, a high standard of living and many attractive neighboring countries to choose from.

191

TRAVEL AND TOURISM

Tourists were estimated to spend nearly US$100 billion in 2004 by the World Travel and Tourism Council (WTTC). This was up 14.7% from the 2003 total and represents 3.8% of the world's gross domestic product (GDP). If all components of the tourist industry were considered, such as investment and government spending, the 2004 total would be about US$1.5 trillion, or 10.4% of the GDP. The year 2004 represented a recovery from a two-year downturn caused by combined effects of the terrorism of September 11 2001 in the USA, the war in Iraq, the SARS disease, mostly in Asia, and the general poor performance of world economies. The rebound was helped by low-cost airlines in Europe and North America. Tourists are also turning more frequently to Internet bookings that offer reduced prices. The box below shows the USA leading in money spent by tourists in 2002. The largest growth in earnings among the leaders were Hong Kong, China and Austria, all with double-digit growth over 2001. In terms of tourist numbers, however, France led with 77 million arrivals, followed by Spain with 51.7 million and the USA with 41.9 million.

TRAVEL AND TOURISM ECONOMY
Percentage of total GDP

- 50 – 93%
- 20 – 49.9%
- 10 – 19.9%
- 6 – 9.9%
- 1 – 5.9%
- No data

TOURIST SPENDING

Top earning destinations, international tourism receipts

Country	(US$billion)	share of total receipts (%)
USA	66.5	14.0
Spain	33.6	7.1
France	32.3	6.8
Italy	26.9	5.7
China	20.4	4.3
Germany	19.2	4.0
UK	17.8	3.8
Austria	11.2	2.4
Hong Kong	10.1	2.1
Greece	9.7	2.1

See pages 8 and 9 for country abbreviations

TRAVEL AND TOURISM JOBS

Percentage of Total Employment

The world's travel and tourist industry was predicted to generate 73,692,500 jobs in 2004. If the broader travel and tourist economy is considered, this total would increase to 214,697,000.

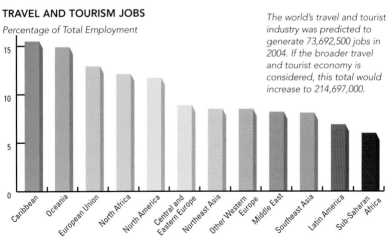

COUNTRY STATISTICS

Countries		Area		Population	Health	
		Area km^2	Area miles^2	Population in thousands	Life expectancy at birth	Infant mortal rate (death. per 1,000 live births)
Afghanistan	AFG	652,090	251,772	28,717	–	142.5
Albania	ALB	28,748	11,100	3,582	72.8	37.3
Algeria	DZA	2,381,741	919,590	32,819	68.9	37.7
American Samoa	ASM	199	77	70	–	9.8
Andorra	AND	468	181	69	–	4.1
Angola	AGO	1,246,700	481,351	10,766	44.6	193.8
Antigua and Barbuda	ATG	442	171	68	–	20.9
Argentina	ARG	2,780,400	1,073,512	38,741	72.9	16.2
Armenia	ARM	29,800	11,506	3,326	72.4	40.9
Aruba	ABW	193	75	71	–	6.1
Australia	AUS	7,741,220	2,988,885	19,732	78.7	4.8
Austria	AUT	83,859	32,378	8,188	77.7	4.3
Azerbaijan	AZE	86,600	33,436	7,831	71.0	82.4
Bahamas	BHS	13,878	5,358	297	69.0	26.2
Bahrain	BHR	694	268	667	72.9	18.6
Bangladesh	BGD	143,998	55,598	138,448	58.1	66.1
Barbados	BRB	430	166	277	–	12.7
Belarus	BLR	207,600	80,154	10,322	68.5	13.9
Belgium	BEL	30,528	11,787	10,289	77.9	4.6
Belize	BLZ	22,966	8,867	266	73.6	27.1
Benin	BEN	112,622	43,483	7,041	53.5	86.8
Bhutan	BTN	47,000	18,147	2,140	60.7	104.7
Bolivia	BOL	1,098,581	424,162	8,586	61.4	56.1
Bosnia-Herzegovina	BIH	51,197	19,767	3,989	–	22.7
Botswana	BWA	581,730	224,606	1,573	44.4	67.3
Brazil	BRA	8,514,215	3,287,338	182,033	67.2	31.7
Brunei	BRN	5,765	2,226	358	75.5	13.5
Bulgaria	BGR	110,912	42,823	7,538	70.8	13.7
Burkina Faso	BFA	274,000	105,791	13,228	45.3	99.8
Burma (Myanmar)	MMR	676,578	261,227	42,511	55.8	70.4
Burundi	BDI	27,834	10,747	6,096	40.6	71.5
Cambodia	KHM	181,035	69,898	13,125	56.5	75.9
Cameroon	CMR	475,442	183,568	15,746	50.0	70.1
Canada	CAN	9,970,610	3,849,653	32,207	78.5	4.9
Cape Verde Islands	CPV	4,033	1,557	412	–	50.5
Cayman Islands	CYM	264	102	42	–	8.6
Central African Republic	CAF	622,984	240,534	3,684	44.3	93.3
Chad	TCD	1,284,000	495,752	9,253	45.2	95.7
Chile	CHL	756,626	292,133	15,665	74.9	8.9
China	CHN	9,596,961	3,705,387	1,286,975	69.8	25.3
Colombia	COL	1,138,914	439,735	41,662	70.4	22.5
Comoros	COM	2,235	863	633	58.8	79.5

Literacy	Wealth	Income*		Unemployment	Automobiles	Media
% 15+ year olds who are illiterate	GDP per capita (PPP US$)	female	male	% labor force unemployed	Automobiles per 1,000 people	Televisions per 1,000 people
–	–	–	–	–	1.3	–
16.3	3,680	2,608	4,705	15.8	29.3	109
34.3	6,090	2,784	9,329	27.3	25.4	105
–	–	–	–	–	–	–
–	2,040	–	–	–	–	–
–	–	–	–	–	17.7	14
–	10,170	–	–	6.0		–
4.2	11,320	6,064	16,786	19.6	135.8	289
2.6	2,650	2,175	3,152	36.4	0.3	218
–	–	–	–	6.5	–	
33.0	25,370	20,830	29,945	6.3	484.9	639
–	26,730	17,940	35,923	4.0	495.5	516
–	3,090	–	–	1.3	38.5	254
5.6	16,270	12,783	19,857	7.7	162.0	–
13.5	16,060	7,578	22,305	–	250.1	–
61.0	1,610	1,153	2,044	3.3	0.5	6
1.3	15,560	11,852	19,496	9.9	228.6	–
1.3	7,620	6,084	9,358	3.0	134.6	314
–	25,520	15,835	35,601	7.5	448.2	510
7.8	5,690	2,188	9,100	12.8	44.2	–
63.6	980	803	1,163	–	6.7	10
–	1,833	–	–	–	–	–
15.6	2,300	1,427	3,181	7.4	29.5	116
–	5,970	–	–	–	27.2	41
23.8	7,820	5,888	9,826	15.8	30.2	20
14.1	7,360	4,391	10,410	9.4	–	316
2.6	19,210	11,716	26,122	–	292.6	–
–	6,890	5,484	8,378	17.6	232.5	398
77.1	1,120	927	1,323	–	3.7	9
–	–	–	–	–	0.6	7
53.0	690	573	814	–	–	4
15.8	1,860	1,621	2,113	1.8	4.3	123
29.7	1,680	1,032	2,338	–	7.2	32
3.9	27,130	20,990	33,391	7.7	459.1	715
27.2	5,570	3,557	7,781	–	8.4	–
–	–	–	–	–	–	–
54.3	1,300	987	1,632	–	0.3	5
58.4	1,070	796	1,350	–	1.5	1
5.2	9,190	5,055	13,409	7.8	88.3	232
–	4,020	3,169	4,825	4.0	3.2	272
–	7,040	4,534	9,608	15.7	43.4	217
45.1	1,870	1,340	2,395	–	18.0	–

Countries		Area		Population	Health	
		Area km^2	Area miles^2	Population in thousands	Life expectancy at birth	Infant mortality rate (deaths per 1,000 live births)
Congo	COG	342,000	132,046	2,954	50.9	95.3
Congo (Democratic Republic of)	COD	2,344,858	905,350	56,625	50.5	96.6
Costa Rica	CRI	51,100	19,730	3,896	76.0	10.6
Croatia	HRV	56,538	21,829	4,422	73.3	6.9
Cuba	CUB	110,861	42,803	11,263	75.7	7.2
Cyprus	CYP	9,251	3,572	772	77.8	7.5
Czech Republic	CZE	78,866	30,450	10,249	74.3	5.4
Denmark	DNK	43,094	16,639	5,384	75.9	4.9
Djibouti	DJI	23,200	8,958	457	45.5	107.0
Dominica	DMA	751	290	70	–	15.3
Dominican Republic	DOM	48,511	18,730	8,716	67.3	34.2
East Timor	TLS	14,874	5,743	998	–	50.5
Ecuador	ECU	283,561	109,483	13,710	69.5	32.0
Egypt	EGY	1,001,449	386,659	74,719	66.3	35.3
El Salvador	SLV	21,041	8,124	6,470	69.1	26.8
Equatorial Guinea	GNQ	28,051	10,830	510	50.0	89.0
Eritrea	ERI	117,600	45,405	4,362	51.5	76.3
Estonia	EST	45,100	17,413	1,409	70.0	12.0
Ethiopia	ETH	1,104,300	426,370	66,558	44.5	103.2
Fiji	FJI	18,274	7,056	869	68.4	13.4
Finland	FIN	338,145	130,558	5,191	77.2	3.7
France	FRA	551,500	212,934	60,181	78.1	4.4
Gabon	GAB	267,668	103,347	1,322	52.4	55.1
Gambia, The	GMB	11,295	4,361	1,501	45.4	74.9
Georgia	GEO	69,700	26,911	4,934	72.7	51.2
Germany	DEU	357,022	137,846	82,398	77.3	4.2
Ghana	GHA	238,533	92,098	20,468	56.3	53.0
Gibraltar	GIB	6	2	28	–	5.3
Greece	GRC	131,957	50,949	10,666	78.0	6.1
Greenland	GRL	2,175,600	839,999	56	–	16.8
Grenada	GRD	344	133	89	–	14.6
Guadeloupe	GLP	1,705	658	440	–	9.1
Guam	GUM	549	212	164	–	6.5
Guatemala	GTM	108,889	42,042	13,909	64.0	37.9
Guinea	GIN	245,857	94,925	9,030	46.5	93.3
Guinea-Bissau	GNB	36,125	13,948	1,361	44.1	110.3
Guyana	GUY	214,969	83,000	702	63.7	37.6
Haiti	HTI	27,750	10,714	7,528	52.0	76.0
Honduras	HND	112,088	43,277	6,670	65.6	30.0
Hong Kong	HKG	1,075	415	7,394	–	5.6
Hungary	HUN	93,032	35,920	10,045	70.7	8.6

Literacy	Wealth	Income*		Unemployment	Automobiles	Media
% 15+ year olds who are illiterate	GDP per capita (PPP US$)	female	male	% labor force unemployed	Automobiles per 1,000 people	Televisions per 1,000 people
20.3	970	695	1,253	–	13.9	12
39.6	680	486	879	–	–	135
5.4	9,460	5,189	13,589	6.1	87.5	387
2.7	9,170	6,612	11,929	14.8	–	272
4.3	5,259	–	–	–	15.6	239
–	21,190	13,513	28,899	3.3	340.8	–
–	14,720	10,555	19,113	7.3	334.7	447
–	29,000	24,086	34,011	4.7	352.9	585
36.4	2,370	–	–	–	15.6	–
–	5,520	–	–	23.1	–	–
17.3	7,020	3,663	10,278	15.9	28.6	95
–	–	–	–	–	–	–
9.4	3,280	1,504	5,040	9.3	40.7	293
45.7	3,520	1,970	5,075	9.0	22.8	122
22.3	5,260	2,771	7,846	6.2	30.0	675
17.8	15,073	–	–	–	3.7	–
45.3	1,030	703	1,361	–	1.6	14
1.2	10,170	7,993	12,720	10.3	330.8	480
61.9	810	550	1,074	–	0.9	5
8.1	4,850	2,507	7,113	5.4	38.7	–
–	24,430	20,234	28,831	9.1	403.2	640
–	23,990	18,607	29,657	8.9	468.8	601
–	5,990	–	–	–	22.4	55
64.4	2,050	1,530	2,581	–	7.5	3
–	2,560	1,507	3,712	12.3	49.3	473
–	25,350	18,474	32,557	8.7	507.9	580
29.4	2,250	1,924	2,579	–	5.1	99
–	–	–	–	–	–	–
3.8	17,440	10,833	24,235	9.6	254.5	466
–	–	–	–	–	–	–
–	6,740	–	–	17.0	–	–
–	–	–	–	19.9	–	–
–	–	–	–	5.5	–	–
32.5	4,400	2,144	6,620	1.8	52.2	126
–	1,960	–	–	–	2.1	41
62.6	970	636	1,313	–	6.5	–
2.5	4,690	2,658	6,844	11.7	–	–
51.2	1,860	1,339	2,396	–	4.4	5
26.0	2,830	1,509	4,131	4.2	52.2	90
–	24,850	18,028	31,883	7.3	58.0	431
–	12,340	9,183	15,803	5.8	238.4	437

Countries		Area		Population	Health	
		Area km²	Area miles²	Population in thousands	Life expectancy at birth	Infant mortality rate (deaths per 1,000 live births)
Iceland	ISL	103,000	39,768	281	78.9	3.5
India	IND	3,287,263	1,269,212	1,049,700	62.3	59.6
Indonesia	IDN	1,904,569	735,354	234,893	65.1	38.1
Iran	IRN	1,648,195	636,368	68,279	68.0	44.2
Iraq	IRQ	438,317	169,234	24,683	–	55.2
Ireland	IRL	70,273	27,132	3,924	76.1	5.3
Israel	ISR	20,600	7,954	6,117	78.3	7.4
Italy	ITA	301,318	116,339	57,998	78.2	6.2
Ivory Coast	CIV	322,463	124,503	16,962	–	–
Jamaica	JAM	10,991	4,244	2,696	74.8	13.3
Japan	JPN	377,829	145,880	127,214	80.5	3.3
Jersey						5.4
Jordan	JOR	89,342	34,495	5,460	69.7	18.9
Kazakhstan	KAZ	2,724,900	1,052,084	16,764	64.1	58.7
Kenya	KEN	580,367	224,080	31,639	52.2	63.4
Korea, North	PRK	120,538	46,540	22,466	–	25.7
Korea, South	KOR	99,268	38,327	48,289	74.3	7.3
Kuwait	KWT	17,818	6,880	2,183	75.9	10.4
Kyrgyzstan	KGZ	199,900	77,181	4,893	66.9	75.3
Laos	LAO	236,800	91,428	5,922	52.5	88.9
Latvia	LVA	64,600	24,942	2,349	69.6	14.6
Lebanon	LBN	10,400	4,015	3,728	72.6	26.4
Lesotho	LSO	30,355	11,720	1,862	51.2	86.2
Liberia	LBR	111,369	43,000	3,317	–	132.2
Libya	LBY	1,759,540	679,358	5,499	70.0	26.8
Liechtenstein	LIE	160	62	33	–	4.9
Lithuania	LTU	65,200	25,174	3,593	71.4	14.2
Luxembourg	LUX	2,586	998	454	77.0	4.7
Macau	MAC	18	7	470	–	4.4
Macedonia, The Former Yugoslav Republic of	MKD	25,713	9,928	2,063	72.7	12.1
Madagascar	MDG	587,041	226,657	16,980	51.6	80.2
Malawi	MWI	118,484	45,747	11,651	–	105.2
Malaysia	MYS	329,758	127,320	23,093	40.7	19.0
Maldives	MDV	298	115	330	71.9	60.1
Mali	MLI	1,240,192	478,838	11,626	–	119.2
Malta	MLT	316	122	400	50.9	5.6
Mauritania	MRT	1,025,520	395,953	2,913	50.5	73.8
Mauritius	MUS	2,040	788	1,210	70.7	16.1
Mexico	MEX	1,958,201	756,061	104,908	72.2	23.7
Moldova	MDA	33,851	13,070	4,440	66.6	41.6
Mongolia	MNG	1,566,500	604,826	2,712	61.9	57.2

Literacy	Wealth	Income*		Unemployment	Automobiles	Media
% 15+ year olds who are illiterate	GDP per capita (PPP US$)	female	male	% labor force unemployed	Automobiles per 1,000 people	Televisions per 1,000 people
–	29,990	23,130	36,799	3.3	545.6	–
43.8	2,840	1,531	4,070	–	4.8	69
14.2	2,940	1,987	3,893	9.1	13.6	136
25.0	6,000	2,599	9,301	12.3	29.9	157
61.7	–	–	–	–	36.3	83
–	32,410	18,701	46,280	3.7	271.8	403
6.2	19,790	13,726	26,011	10.3	219.7	318
2.6	24,670	15,452	34,460	9.0	538.9	486
–	–	792	2,160	–	20.5	70
14.1	3,720	2,969	4,492	15.8	41.0	182
–	25,130	15,617	35,061	5.4	394.7	707
–	–	–	–	–	–	–
11.2	3,870	1,771	5,800	–	49.5	52
1.6	6,500	5,039	8,077	13.7	66.2	231
18.6	980	930	1,031	–	10.2	21
–	–	–	–	–	–	53
3.2	15,090	9,529	20,578	3.1	167.3	346
19.1	18,700	8,605	25,333	–	317.0	491
–	2,750	–	–	–	38.5	45
36.2	1,620	1,278	1,962	–	3.4	4
1.2	7,730	6,470	9,215	12.0	218.1	492
15.0	4,170	1,963	6,472	–	313.4	352
17.6	2,420	1,375	3,620	–	6.6	25
47.5	–	–	–	–	3.3	–
21.1	7,570	–	–	–	166.9	126
–	–	–	–	–	–	–
1.4	8,470	6,843	10,326	13.8	294.5	459
–	53,780	29,569	78,723	3.0	586.6	–
–	–	–	–	6.3	110.1	–
–	6,110	–	–	31.9	138.5	250
34.5	830	616	1,046	–	4.4	21
40.9	570	464	679	–	2.9	2
13.6	8,750	5,557	11,845	3.8	169.6	166
4.1	4,798	–	–		4.3	–
75.4	810	615	1,009		2.7	12
9.0	13,160	6,787	19,647	6.8	454.6	–
60.8	1,990	1,429	2,566	–	8.0	21
16.5	9,860	5,273	14,497	9.7	72.5	226
9.8	8,430	4,637	12,358	1.9	101.9	261
2.1	2,150	1,714	2,626	6.8	54.1	297
2.6	1,740	1,398	2,082	4.6	16.8	63

COUNTRY STATISTICS

Countries		Area		Population	Health	
		Area km^2	Area miles^2	Population in thousands	Life expectancy at birth	Infant mortality rate (deaths per 1,000 live births)
Morocco	MAR	446,550	172,413	31,689	66.6	44.9
Mozambique	MOZ	801,590	309,494	17,479	40.6	199.0
Namibia	NAM	824,292	318,259	1,927	45.1	68.4
Nepal	NPL	147,181	56,827	26,470	57.3	70.6
Netherlands	NLD	41,526	16,033	16,151	77.9	4.3
Netherlands Antilles	ANT	800	309	216	–	10.7
New Zealand	NZL	270,534	104,453	3,951	77.2	6.1
Nicaragua	NIC	130,000	50,193	5,129	67.7	31.4
Niger	NER	1,267,000	489,189	11,059	44.2	123.6
Nigeria	NGA	923,768	356,667	133,882	51.3	71.4
Norway	NOR	323,877	125,049	4,546	78.1	3.9
Oman	OMN	309,500	119,498	2,807	70.5	21.0
Pakistan	PAK	796,095	307,372	150,695	59.0	76.5
Panama	PAN	75,517	29,157	2,961	73.6	21.4
Papua New Guinea	PNG	462,840	178,703	5,296	55.6	54.8
Paraguay	PRY	406,752	157,047	6,037	69.6	27.7
Peru	PER	1,285,216	496,222	28,410	68.0	37.0
Philippines	PHL	300,000	115,830	84,620	68.6	25.0
Poland	POL	323,250	124,807	38,623	72.8	9.0
Portugal	PRT	88,797	34,285	10,102	75.2	5.7
Puerto Rico	PRI	8,875	3,427	3,886	–	9.4
Qatar	QAT	11,000	4,247	817	68.9	20.0
Romania	ROU	238,391	92,043	22,272	69.8	18.4
Russia	RUS	17,075,400	6,592,812	144,526	66.1	19.5
Rwanda	RWA	26,338	10,169	7,810	39.4	102.6
Samoa	WSM	2,831	1,093	178	68.5	29.7
San Marino	SMR	61	24	28	–	6.0
São Tomé and Príncipe	STP	964	372	176	–	46.0
Saudi Arabia	SAU	2,149,690	829,995	24,294	70.9	47.9
Senegal	SEN	196,722	75,954	10,580	52.3	57.6
Serbia and Montenegro	SCG	102,173	39,449	10,656	–	65.0
Seychelles	SYC	455	176	80	–	16.4
Sierra Leone	SLE	71,740	27,699	5,733	37.3	146.9
Singapore	SGP	683	264	4,609	77.1	3.6
Slovak Republic	SVK	49,012	18,924	5,430	72.8	8.6
Slovenia	SVN	20,256	7,821	1,936	75.0	4.4
Solomon Islands	SLB	28,896	11,157	509	67.4	22.9
Somalia	SOM	637,657	246,199	8,025	–	120.3
South Africa	ZAF	1,221,037	471,442	42,769	56.7	60.8
Spain	ESP	497,548	192,103	40,217	78.1	4.5
Sri Lanka	LKA	65,610	25,332	19,742	71.6	15.2
St Kitts and Nevis	KNA	261	101	39	–	15.4

Literacy	Wealth	Income*		Unemployment	Automobiles	Media
% 15+ year olds who are illiterate	GDP per capita (PPP US$)	female	male	% labor force unemployed	Automobiles per 1,000 people	Televisions per 1,000 people
52.2	3,600	2,057	5,139	11.6	41.1	160
57	1,140	916	1,382	–	0.3	5
19	7,120	4,833	9,511	33.8	46.4	37
59.3	1,310	867	1,734	–	–	6
–	27,190	18,846	35,675	2.7	382.9	543
4.5	–	–	–	14.0	–	–
–	19,160	15,524	22,900	5.2	480.5	508
34.5	2,450	1,494	3,415	12.2	2.6	190
85	890	646	1,129	–	4.1	27
37	850	505	1,191	–	7.7	66
–	–	23,317	36,043	3.9	406.6	579
29.3	12,040	3,919	17,960	–	97.1	595
57.8	1,890	909	2,824	7.8	5.0	88
9.1	5,750	3,399	8,056	11.8	82.8	187
37.1	2,570	1,865	3,231	–	6.7	24
7.7	5,210	2,548	7,832	8.2	14.3	101
11.1	4,570	1,903	7,206	7.9	27.1	144
6.1	3,840	2,838	4,829	9.8	10.3	108
1.3	9,450	7,253	11,777	19.9	240.2	413
8.8	18,150	12,782	23,940	5.1	309.7	542
–	–	–	–	12.3	232.1	271
19.8	19,844	–	–	–	244.7	–
2.9	5,830	4,313	7,416	8.4	133.3	233
1.4	7,100	5,609	8,795	13.4	119.7	420
34.2	1,250	965	1,567	–	1.9	0
2.4	1,317	–	–	–	–	–
–	6,180	–	–	3.6	–	–
–	–	–	–	–	29.6	–
24.8	13,330	4,222	21,141	4.6	93.3	262
63.6	1,500	1,065	1,941	–	10.0	41
–	–	–	–	13.8	175.5	259
–	17,030	–	–	–	93.2	–
–	470	–	–	–	4.5	13
–	22,680	14,992	30,262	5.2	96.9	348
–	11,960	9,468	14,595	18.5	229.2	402
91.4	17,130	13,152	21,338	5.9	417.9	356
–	1,910	–	–	–	–	–
–	–	–	–	–	0.1	–
15.8	11,290	7,047	15,712	5.4	94.2	125
3.4	20,150	12,331	28,275	11.4	389.0	506
9.4	3,180	2,095	4,189	8.7	15.1	92
–	11,300	–	–	–	–	–

COUNTRY STATISTICS

Countries		Area Area km^2	Area miles^2	Population Population in thousands	Health Life expectancy at birth	Infant mortality rate (deaths per 1,000 live births)
St Lucia	LCA	539	208	162	–	14.4
St Vincent and the Grenadines	VCT	388	150	117	–	15.7
Sudan	SDN	2,505,813	967,494	38,114	55.0	65.6
Suriname	SUR	163,265	63,037	435	70.1	24.7
Swaziland	SWZ	17,364	6,704	1,161	50.8	67.4
Sweden	SWE	449,964	173,731	8,878	79.3	3.4
Switzerland	CHE	41,284	15,940	7,319	78.6	4.4
Syria	SYR	185,180	71,498	17,586	70.5	31.7
Tajikistan	TJK	143,100	55,251	6,864	67.2	113.4
Tanzania	TZA	945,090	364,899	35,922	51.1	103.7
Thailand	THA	513,115	198,114	64,265	69.9	21.8
Togo	TGO	56,785	21,925	5,429	51.3	68.7
Tonga	TON	650	251	108	–	13.4
Trinidad and Tobago	TTO	5,130	1,981	1,104	73.8	25.0
Tunisia	TUN	163,610	63,170	9,925	69.5	26.9
Turkey	TUR	774,815	299,156	68,109	69.0	44.2
Turkmenistan	TKM	488,100	188,455	4,776	65.4	73.2
Uganda	UGA	241,038	93,065	25,633	41.9	87.9
Ukraine	UKR	603,700	233,089	48,055	68.1	20.9
United Arab Emirates	ARE	83,600	32,278	2,485	74.6	15.6
United Kingdom	GBR	241,857	93,381	60,095	77.2	5.3
United States of America	USA	9,629,091	3,717,792	290,343	76.5	6.4
Uruguay	URY	175,016	67,574	3,413	73.9	13.8
Uzbekistan	UZB	447,400	172,741	25,982	68.3	71.5
Vanuatu	VUT	12,189	4,706	199	–	58.1
Venezuela	VEN	912,050	352,143	24,655	72.4	23.79
Vietnam	VNM	331,689	128,065	81,625	67.2	30.8
Yemen	YEM	527,968	203,848	19,350	59.4	–
Zambia	ZMB	752,618	290,586	10,307	40.5	99.3
Zimbabwe	ZWE	390,757	150,871	12,577	42.9	66.5

*Estimated earned income (PPP US$, 2001)

Literacy	Wealth	Income*		Unemployment	Automobiles	Media
% 15+ year olds who are illiterate	GDP per capita (PPP US$)	female	male	% labor force unemployed	Automobiles per 1,000 people 2003	Televisions per 1,000 people
–	5,260	–	–	20.5	98.9	–
–	5,330	–	–	19.8	–	–
43.3	1,970	935	2,992	–	9.9	87
–	4,599	–	–	14.0	122.5	–
21.4	4,330	2,395	6,453	–	34.4	–
–	24,180	19,636	28,817	4.0	436.6	531
–	28,100	18,782	37,619	2.9	485.6	535
26.6	3,280	1,423	5,109	11.7	9.0	70
1.8	1,170	891	1,451	2.7	0.1	285
26.0	520	432	610	–	0.8	21
5.5	6,400	4,875	7,975	2.6	28.2	236
43.9	1,650	1,058	2,254	–	19.7	18
–	–	–	–	–	11.7	–
2.7	9,100	5,645	12,614	10.8	96.1	334
30.0	6,390	3,377	9,359	15.6	29.6	198
16.0	5,890	3,717	8,028	10.6	63.3	286
–	4,320	–	–	–	–	201
34.0	1,490	1,185	1,799	–	2.2	27
1.4	4,350	3,071	5,826	10.2	104.4	490
24.8	20,530	6,041	28,223	2.3	81.8	294
–	24,160	18,180	30,476	5.1	373.2	645
–	34,320	26,389	42,540	5.8	477.8	847
3.4	8,400	5,774	11,190	15.3	158.3	241
1.8	2,460	1,951	2,976	0.4	–	275
–	3,190	–	–	–	23.1	–
8.5	5,670	3,288	8,021	15.8	68.1	185
8.5	2,070	1,696	2,447	11.5	–	47
54.6	790	365	1,201	–	15.3	29
22.8	780	554	1,009	–	17.0	137
12.3	2,280	1,667	2,905	–	27.6	30

Credits

12–13
Map: International Union for Conservation of Nature and Natural Resources (IUCN), Red List 2003
Bottom right: United Nations Environment Programme (UNEP), Secretariat of the Convention on Biological Diversity, *Global Diversity Outlook*

14–15
IUCN Red List 2003

16–17
Food and Agriculture Organization of the United Nations (FAO)
Top left: Environmental Defense, *Business Guide to Sustainable Seafood/* Audobon

18–19
Map: various sources
Bottom right: Landsat Project/USGS

20–21
Map: Carbon Dioxide Information Analysis Center (CDIAC) 1998
Bottom right: The Met Office, The Hadley Centre
Left: JPL/NASA

22–23
Map: various sources
Top: World Bank, *World Development Indicators* 2002, (1995–1998 data)
Bottom right: Greg Shirah/GSFC/NASA

24–25
Map: various sources
Bottom left: United Nations Joint Group of Experts on the Scientific Aspects of Marine Environmental Protection (GESAMP)
Top left: International Association of Independent Tanker Owners (INTERTANKO)
Bottom right: World Bank, *World Development Indicators* 2001
Center for Environmental Systems Research, University of Kassel, Water Gap 2.1 2000

26–27
Philip's research

28–29
Philip's research
Top left: RSD/GSFC/NASA

32–33
US Bureau of the Census, International Data Base, (midyear 2003)

34–35
US Bureau of the Census, International Data Base, (latest available year)

36–37
United Nations Population Division (UNPD)

38–39
UNPD
World Urbanization Prospects: The 2001 Revision (2000 data)

40–41
Various sources
Bottom left: ISS Crew/Earth Sciences and Image Analysis Lab, JSC/NASA

44–45
Various sources

46–47
Map: Philip's research (2001 data)
Key: Unrepresented Nations and Peoples Organisation (UNPO)

48–49
Map: Philip's research (2001 data)
Bottom: http://www.adherents. com/

50–51
Various sources
Bottom left: 1999 data

54–55
Map: based on CIA Factbook 2003, but updated
Bottom: International Institute for Democracy and Electoral Assistance (IDEA),
Voter Turnout Since 1945: A Global Report 2001

56–57
United Nations Development Programme (UNDP), *Human Development Report* 2003

58–59
Philip's research
Bottom right: UN 2001

68–69
United Nations Office on Drugs and Crime (UNODC): 7th Survey, (latest available year, 1996–2000)

70–71
Amnesty International, (2002 data)

72–73
Interpol International Crime Statistics, (latest available year)

74–75
UNODC, (1994–2000 data)

76–77
UNODC, *World Drug Report* 2000

80–81
Map: Philip's research
Bottom right: *Journal of Peace Research* (2003), Nils Petter Gleditsch and Bethany Lacina, Centre for the Study of Civil War, International Peace Research Institute, Oslo (PRIO).
For more information *see* www.prio.no/cwp/Armed Conflict

82–83
United Nations High Commissioner on Refugees (UNHCR), *Refugees and Others of Concern to UNHCR: Statistical Overview* (1999)

84–85
Map: UNDP, *Human Development Report* 2003
Bottom left: Center for Defense Information (CDI) (2004 data)
Bottom right: www.globalsecurity.org (2003 data)

86–87
US Department of State (1999 data)

88–89
Terrorist Groups: Various sources including US Department of State list
Major Terrorist attacks: International Policy Institute for Counter-Terrorism (ICT), International Terrorism database

90–91
Map + bottom right: UNHCR, (2003 data)
Bottom left: UNHCR, *Refugees by Numbers* (2003)

94–95
UNDP, *Human Development Report* 2002/2003
Bottom: WHO

96–97
World Health Organization (WHO), *WHO Regional Immunization Profiles* (2002)
Bottom right: WHO, *The World Health Report* 2001

98–99
Map: UNDP *Human Development Report* 2003 (2001/2002 data)
Bottom left: CIA Factbook 2001
Bottom right: Joint United Aids Programme on HIV/AIDS (UNAIDS) 2003 *AIDS Epidemic Update December 2003*

100–101
Map: UNDP, *Human Development Report* 2003 (1992–2000 data)
Bottom left: WHO (1998–99 data)
Bottom right: WHO, Global Alcohol Database (2000 data)

102–103
AQUASTAT/WHO (2000 data)

104–105
Map: UN *Statistical Year book* 2000
Bottom right: FAO, *The State of Food Insecurity in the World* 2000

108–109
Map: United Nations Educational, Scientific

and Cultural Organization
(UNESCO), Institute for
Statistics, (2001 data)
Bottom right: UNESCO,
*EFA Global Monitoring
Report 2002*

110–111
UNESCO
(2000–2001 data)

112–113
UNESCO

114–115
United Nations Children's
Fund (UNICEF),
*The State of the World's
Children 2004*
Key: Human Rights Watch
http://www.hrw.org/
1999–2001 data)

118–119
Map and bottom left:
UNDP,
*Human Development
Report 2003* (2001 data)
Bottom right: World Bank,
*World Development
Indicators 2004*

120–121
World Bank,
*World Development
Indicators 2001*

122–123
International Monetary
Fund (IMF),
*The World Economic
Outlook (WEO) 2000*

124–125
Left: UNDP,
*Human Development
Report 2003* (2001 data)
Right: World Bank, *World
Development Indicators
2003* (2001 data)

128–129
Various sources (2000)

130–131
Various sources (2000)

132–133
Various sources (2000)

134–135
IA export figures 2000

136–137
Various sources including:
The International
Organization of Motor
Vehicle Manufacturers
(OICA)

World Bank,
*World Development
Indicators 2004,*
(1998–2002 data)

138–139
Institute of Shipping
Economics and
Logistics (ISL),
*Shipping Statistics
Yearbook 2001*
(latest available year)

140–141
International Monetary
Fund (IMF),
*Global Financial Stability
Report – Market
Developments and
Issues 2004,*
(2000–2002 data)
Top left:
World Bank, *World
Development Indicators
2002*

142–143
UN Conference on Trade
and Development
*World Investment Report
2003,* (2001/2002 data)

144–145
FAO/CIA
(latest available year)

146–147
UNDP,
*Human Development
Report 2003*
Bottom right: UNSTATS
*World's Women 2000:
Trends and Statistics*

150–151
Map: various sources
Bottom right:
based on FAO land use
data (2001)

152–153
Various sources
(2000 data)

154–155
Map: various sources
(latest available year)
Bottom right: FAO

156–157
FAOSTAT (2000 data)

160–161
Map: Electronic
Industries Alliance (EIA)
(2000 data)
Bottom:
BP *Statistical Review of
World Energy 2001*

162–163
BP, *Statistical Review of
World Energy 2001*

164–165
International Energy
Agency (IEA), *IEA Energy
Balances 2003*
Top right: BP, *Statistical
Review of World Energy
2001/EIA*

166–167
Various sources

168–169
USGS Mineral
Commodity Summaries
(2000 data)

172–174
International
Telecommunication
Union (ITU), *World
Telecommunication
Report 1999*

174–175
ITU 2002

176–177
Map: ITU 2003
Bottom left: World Bank,
*World Development
Indicators 2002*

178–179
UNESCO,
World Culture Report
Bottom right: UNESCO

180–181
IFPI,
*The Recording Industry
World Sales 2002*

182–183
UNESCO,
World Culture Report
Bottom left:
Confederation of Indian
Industry (CII)

184–185
International Olympic
Committee

186–187
Map: FIFA, *Big Count,
Football Worldwide 2000*
Bottom right: FIFA

188–189
Map: World Tourism
Organization (WTO)/CIA
(1999–2001 data)
Bottom right: Airports
Council International
(ACI) (2002 data)

190–191
World Tourism
Organization (WTO),
Highlights 2002

192–193
World Travel and
Tourism Council (WTTC),
World at a glance 2004

194–203
Area: Philip's
Population:
CIA 2003 estimates
Life Expectancy: UNDP,
*Human Development
Report 2002*
Infant mortality: WHO
Literacy: UNESCO EFA,
*Global Monitoring
Report 2002*
GDP per capita: UNDP,
*Human Development
Report 2003*
Salary male/female:
UNDP,
*Human Development
Report 2003*
Unemployment:
International Labour
Office (ILO)
Automobiles per 1,000:
World Bank,
*World Development
Indicators 2001*
Televisions: International
Telecommunication
Union (ITU), *World
Telecommunication
Report 1999*

Websites

Listed below is a selection of international websites
providing information relating to the state of the world

**Food and Agriculture Organization of the United
Nations (FAO)**
http://www.fao.org/

International Energy Agency (IEA)
http://www.iea.org/

International Labour Organization
http://www.ilo.org/

International Monetary Fund (IMF)
http://www.imf.org/

International Telecommunication Union (ITU)
http://www.itu.int/home/

**International Union for Conservation of Nature and
Natural Resources (IUCN)**
http://www.iucn.org/

Joint United Nations Programme on HIV/AIDS
http://www.unaids.org/

United Nations Children Fund (UNICEF)
http://www.unicef.org/

United Nations Development Programme (UNDP)
http://www.undp.org/

**United Nations Educational, Scientific and Cultural
Organization (UNESCO)**
http://www.unesco.org/

United Nations Environment Programme (UNEP)
http://www.unep.org/

**United Nations High Commissioner on Refugees
(UNHCR)**
http://www.unhcr.ch/cgi-bin/texis/vtx/home

United Nations Office on Drugs and Crime (UNODC)
http://www.unodc.org/unodc/index.html

United Nations Population Division
http://www.un.org/esa/population/unpop.htm

World Bank
http://www.worldbank.org/

World Health Organization (WHO)
http://www.who.int/en/

World Tourism Organization (WTO)
http://www.world-tourism.org/

World Travel and Tourism Council (WTTC)
http://www.wttc.org/

Chapter introduction picture credits

10–11 Tail of surfacing Humpback Whale, near
Kupreanof Island, Alaska, USA.
Paul A. Souders/*Corbis*

30–31 Busy New York street, New York, USA.
Mark L. Stephenson/*Corbis*

42–43 Crowd at Macy's Thanksgiving Day Parade,
New York, USA.
Joseph Sohm; ChromoSohm Inc./*Corbis*

52–53 European Union flags at European Parliament
in Strasbourg.
Vincent Kessler/Reuters/*Corbis*

66–67 Unlocking jail cell.
Charles O'Rear/*Corbis*

78–79 U.S. Soldiers in gas masks and rain suits,
Operation Desert Shield, Saudi Arabia, 1991.
Corbis

92–93 A man drinks from a new UNICEF well in
Vahun, Liberia, western Africa.
Liba Taylor/*Corbis*

106–107 Blue Hmong tribal children in a classroom,
Nong Hoi, Thailand.
Lindsay Hebberd/*Corbis*

116–117 Stacks of gold bars.
Craig Aurness/*Corbis*

126–127 Automated automobile assembly line,
Durban, South Africa.
Charles O'Rear/*Corbis*

148–149 Wheat harvesting, Washington state, USA.
Terry W. Eggers/*Corbis*

158–159 Windmill at sunrise, Idaho, USA.
Darrell Gulin/*Corbis*

170–171 A jet airliner flies into the sunset at Los
Angeles International Airport, California, USA.
Joseph Sohm; ChromoSohm Inc./*Corbis*

Index

INDEX